A Short History of Manitoba

Ed Whitcomb

Canadian Cataloguing in Publication Data

Whitcomb, Edward A.
A short history of Manitoba

Includes index.
ISBN 0-920002-15-3

1. Manitoba--History. I. Title.

FC3361.W48   971.27   C82-090075-3
F1063.W48

© Canada's Wings, Inc. 1982
Box 393, Stittsville, Ontario
Canada K0A 3G0

Printed in Canada

Contents

Preface

The idea for this book first arose in 1969 when I moved to Nova Scotia. Being new to the province, and knowing very little about it, I went looking for a short history book which would provide an outline of the development of my newly-adopted home. There was no such book. In 1973 I moved to Quebec, later to Ontario, and in neither place could I find a short and simple account of the provinces' development. In 1975 I decided to write the sort of book I had been looking for, and what better place to start than with my native province, Manitoba.

The result is this short history of Manitoba. It is deliberately designed as an inexpensive pamphlet that can be read in a few hours—anyone desiring more detail will benefit from *Manitoba: a History* by W.L. Morton or *A Centennial History of Manitoba* by James A. Jackson. This book briefly outlines exploration and the fur trade, the settlers, the problems they faced and their influence on the province, and early economic and political developments including the struggle over borders, railways, tariffs, and schools. It explains the reasons for the boom that preceded the First World War and the depression that followed, including such issues as scandals, prohibition, women's suffrage, the Winnipeg General Strike, and the rise to power of the farmers' movement. The Depression, and more importantly, its long-term effects are explained, including the efforts of provincial governments since the mid-1950s to foster social and economic development.

Every historian has a point of view that determines which of the thousands of issues he will discuss, which of the millions of facts he will relate, and what things he will emphasize or ignore. This is essentially a political history, with some reference to economic and social developments, and it clearly emphasizes provincial rather than national or local developments. It seeks to explain Manitoba's side in the many disputes between the province and the federal government, a reasonable point of view to take in a book about a province. It is not "romantic" history, and a few unpleasant things are said about some of the heroes, politicians, and groups who have shaped the province. In short, it is but one perspective on a very fascinating and complex society, and my greatest hope is that this small book will encourage others to read more and to write more on the dozens of issues and perspectives necessary to obtain a full understanding of any society's development.

Over the past few years a great many people have helped with this project. Advice and encouragement have been received from academics, archivists, and librarians, from publishers, printers, and booksellers, from politicians and civil servants, and from friends and relatives. Over a dozen people read the entire manuscript providing major improvements to the text and eliminating numerous errors of fact. The list of those who helped is far too long to print here, and it would be completely unfair to single out a few for mention. I can only thank them all with these few general words and hope they will see in this book some small reward for their efforts and kindness. Only two exceptions will be made, to acknowledge my special thanks to the editor, Carl Vincent, and his assistant, Heather Ebbs, whose efforts have made possible publication in time for the centennials of Oak Lake, Brandon, and Neepawa, the respective home towns of myself, my wife, and my mother. I alone am responsible for whatever weaknesses remain in the book.

Uncertain Beginnings
1600—1850

New France, New England, Nova Scotia, all are well known, but few people know that Manitoba began as New Wales. The name was bestowed by a Welshman, Thomas Button, the first white man to discover the province. He spent the frigid winter of 1612-13 at the mouth of the Nelson River, named for his navigator who, like so many of the crew, died of scurvy. The name New Wales soon disappeared from the maps, to be replaced eventually by the name Manitoba. Its origin is Indian, from the windy place near the narrows of Lake Manitoba where, so the Indians believed, the Great Spirit Manitou whispered. It was a fitting change, for surely 10,000 years of habitation by the Indians gave them the right to originate the name.

The term "prairie province" is almost as great a misnomer as New Wales would have been, for most of the province is in the Canadian Shield, a land of ancient rock, lake, river, and muskeg, covered with a variety of trees which never reach great height due to the rigours of the climate. This was an area rich in furs, and it was the fur trade that initially led to exploration and development by the Europeans.

The French had pushed steadily westward from New France (Quebec) until inevitably they heard of a northern or inland sea. By 1660 the French explorers and fur traders Pierre-Esprit Radisson and Médard de Groseilliers had concluded that the Northern Sea the Indians spoke of must by the bay that Henry Hudson had explored in the early seventeenth century and which bore his name. If so, it would be far easier to sail directly into it from the north than to attempt to conduct the fur trade overland from Montreal. After being ignored and mistreated at Quebec, Radisson and Groseilliers convinced the enterprising English of the advantages of conducting the fur trade directly from Hudson Bay.

The initial trip paid off handsomely. On May 2, 1670, King Charles II of England granted to the Hudson's Bay Company (HBC) a monopoly charter on the trade from all land draining into Hudson Bay—almost one-quarter of North America including the whole of Manitoba. The area was named Rupert's Land after the King's cousin. For two centuries the fur trade and the HBC would be dominant factors in the Manitoban economy, and most of Manitoba's trade with Europe would go over the Hudson Bay route. Manitobans have never lost the vision of this northern gateway to the world.

The English began building forts at the mouths of the rivers flowing into the Bay. In the absence of serious competition there was no need to move inland as the Indians willingly came to the coast once they learned of European goods. In fact, the only real attempt the English made to explore this quarter of the continent occurred when Henry Kelsey was sent up the Nelson River in the 1690s. He became the first white man to see the prairies, and the only one to visit there for half a century. He also saw the buffalo, the basis of the prairie economy. It provided nearly everything the plains Indian needed: food, hides for clothing and shelter, bindings, bone for tools and weapons, sinew for thread, and manure for fuel, the latter of great importance on the treeless plains. The spring and autumn buffalo hunts were one of the main activities in Manitoba as long as the Indians, the Métis, and the fur trade dominated. The buffalo meat was cut in strips, dried, beaten to a pulp, mixed with melted fat and sometimes berries to produce pemmican, an enormously nourishing food which could be readily carried and stored for years: rightfully the buffalo is Manitoba's symbol.

The English forts on the Bay were the object of numerous attacks during the many wars between England and France in the seventeenth and eighteenth centuries, and the area changed hands many times. Finally, the Peace of Utrecht in 1713 left Hudson Bay firmly in English hands. The HBC reaped large profits with little effort until 1731, when the French launched an attempt to outflank the English by developing an overland route from Montreal. The task of weaning the Western fur trade from the English fell to a native of New France, Pierre La Verendrye, who had been trading in the Lake Superior region for years. He faced enormous odds, including greater distance and inferior trade goods. Yet he was driven on by motives that were more than just economic, for like the other French explorers he sought to broaden knowledge of the continent, to discover an overland route to the Western Sea (Pacific Ocean), and to bring glory to his King and souls to the Church. From his base on Lake Superior he established Fort St. Pierre on Rainy Lake in 1731, Fort St. Charles on Lake of the Woods in 1732, and Fort Maurepas on the Red River in 1734. Fort Rouge was erected soon after, on the site of the modern city of Winnipeg, and Fort La Reine near present-day Portage la Prairie.

From the Red and Assiniboine Rivers La Verendrye explored south and west to the Missouri which, to his profound regret, flowed southward and not to any Western Sea. On his return to southern Manitoba, La Verendrye founded Fort Dauphin by Lake Winnipegosis and Fort Bourbon where the Saskatchewan River enters Lake Winnipeg. Although he rendered great service as an explorer, La Verendrye failed to find the Western Sea, and, by identifying the vastness of the prairies, made such a possibility seem even more hopeless. It would be another half-century before white men would reach the Pacific by land. Although some furs went to Montreal, the French exploration of the West in the mid-eighteenth century did not seriously weaken the power of the HBC, for the French were too weak and their goods too expensive to offer serious competition to a British company. Only another British company could do that, and it was not long in coming.

The English conquest of Quebec in 1760 triggered a series of events that led to the competition for and hence the opening up of Manitoba. The Scots and Yankee businessmen who arrived in Quebec after 1760 found the French fur trade system virtually intact. It had always enjoyed certain advantages over English competition, especially greater familiarity with the woods and friendship with the Indians. The English had always benefitted from better goods, larger financial resources, and access to richer markets. In the 1800s the Montreal-based North-West Company (NWC) managed to combine the advantages of the English and French systems and eliminate competition in Montreal. It quickly moved into Manitoba and on to the Arctic and Pacific, aided by the work of such great explorers as Peter Pond, David Thompson, Joseph Frobisher, and Simon Fraser. Establishing a string of posts as far as the Rockies, the NWC quickly captured much of the trade of the prairies and of the lower reaches of the Canadian Shield.

The HBC responded to this challenge by sending agents inland and establishing forts. Cumberland House on the Saskatchewan River was followed by a series of posts across the prairies, often side-by-side with the NWC posts. The increasing number of traders and personnel for the forts created a requirement for a permanent supply of food, which led to the development of agriculture as grains, vegetables, and cattle began to be raised near the posts. For a short period the competiton was relatively friendly, as there were plenty of furs and white companionship was a scarce commodity on the plains. But competition inevitably became fierce, and trouble eventually erupted at Red River, the crossroads of the two competing systems and the centre of the vital pemmican supply.

A few white settlers had settled down with their Indian wives to begin permanent settlement near the confluence of the Assiniboine and Red Rivers. The children of the Frenchmen were known as Métis, those of the English as half-breeds. These people remained more closely integrated with the fur trade than agriculture. The first real settlers came from Scotland in 1812. They did so because of the humanitarian ideals of a Scottish nobleman, Lord Thomas, the Earl of Selkirk, who sought to provide at his own expense a new home for the helpless and homeless farmers who were being driven from their land in Scotland. Selkirk could have sent them to Upper Canada (Ontario) or the Maritimes where thousands of refugees and immigrants were settling with little difficulty, but there he could not control the settlement himself, appoint the leaders, provide all the things that were needed, and be the permanent "laird". He was an idealist, but he was also a proud, egotistical aristocrat. His ostensible reason for deciding on the Red River was that the land was rich and the fur trade provided a market for the produce. But the climate was harsh, the valley subject to floods, the agricultural conditions unlike those of Western Europe, and the colony almost totally isolated from world commerce. And if two centuries of North American history had suggested any lesson, it was that settlement was incompatible with the fur trade. The HBC was opposed to the colony from the first, and Selkirk expended a large portion of his fortune trying to overcome its hostility. The opposition of the NWC was more violent, for its overland route depended on the supply of pemmican and a colony at Red River would seriously threaten that supply. For the NWC Selkirk's colony was a matter of life or death; it was to be Selkirk's colonists who died.

In June 1811, thirty-six settlers set out from England for Red River under the command of Miles Macdonnell. After spending a harsh winter at York Factory near the mouth of the Nelson River, they arrived at the Red River in the late summer of 1812 and were later joined by two more groups of settlers. The worst fears of the NWC were almost immediately realized when Macdonnell attempted to gain complete control of the colony by banning the export of pemmican, ordering traders out of the colony, and entering the NWC forts to seize arms, ammunition, and pemmican. The NWC offered free land and safe passage to any settlers who wished to relocate in Central Canada. Many did so. The rest the NWC determined to drive out by burning barns and houses and destroying the first crops. The remaining sixty settlers fled north to Lake Winnipeg, but a new group of colonists who had arrived from Scotland by way of Hudson Bay joined the refugees at Lake Winnipeg, and all returned to harvest good crops and spend a reasonably comfortable winter.

The new governor of the little colony, Robert Semple, chose to ignore all advice about the developing hostility of the Métis, Indians, and fur traders. When finally convinced of the danger, Semple occupied Forts Brandon and Pembina and destroyed Fort Gibraltar in present-day Winnipeg. Although he chose to think these measures made his position more secure, they had the reverse effect because they convinced the Métis, with reason, that the settlers were going to destroy their way of life. In June of 1816 a party of Indians, Métis, and half-breeds approached Fort Douglas near a place called Seven Oaks. They were mounted, armed, experienced as hunters, and commanded by the able and intelligent Cuthbert Grant. The settlers were on foot, unaccustomed to arms, and led by the incompetent Semple. The only advantages Semple had were in his fort, his cannon, and larger numbers. He abandoned the fort and the cannon and walked out to meet the Métis with so few settlers that his group was outnumbered. They were, of course, massacred.

While the Métis and the Nor'Westers were celebrating their victory, Selkirk was approaching from Montreal with a private army of European mercenaries. He seized Fort William from the NWC and found enough evidence of illegal actions by the Nor'Westers to keep the courts busy for years. The seizure and the amount of compensation he paid for the supplies provided the NWC in turn with sufficient allegations against Selkirk to keep the matter before the courts for years. The expenses of buying shares in the HBC, of the settlement, the private army, and the legal battles eventually ruined Selkirk. For the NWC the litigation with both the HBC and Selkirk was one of the costs of competition which, added to price wars, over-trapping, and duplication of forts and transportation systems, finally forced it to terms with the HBC. By the agreement of 1821 the HBC name alone survived; its charter determined the trade; and although each company would provide half the capital and reap half the profits, four of the six managers were HBC men. The overland route to Montreal, always less economical, was abandoned for the shorter Hudson Bay route. Once more the West was cut off from the Canadas.

While the fur trade rivalry was moving to a solution, Selkirk had visited and re-organized his colony. Lots were laid out with 220 yards of river front, one mile of depth, and a second mile for hay or wood. Land was set aside for schools and churches, and plans were made for mills, roads, and bridges. With the hostilities of the fur companies overcome, the chief obstacle became the climate. To the rigours of winter were added plagues of grasshoppers which in 1818 and 1819 ate not only the crops but the leaves and even the bark off trees. Further plagues of insects and mice afflicted the colony. Worse than this climate, with its late frosts in spring and early ones in autumn, were the dry spells which brought drought and prairie fires and the wet periods which brought floods. The worst flood descended in 1826, covering parts of present-day Winnipeg to a depth of fifteen feet, turning the Red River into a lake, and carrying away almost all the houses, barns, and possessions of the colonists. In spite of these problems, the people learned how to survive and a colony slowly began to develop.

The diversity of Manitoba was in the Red River colony from the start. White, Indian, Métis, and half-breed, Catholic and Protestant shared a society based on agriculture, hunting, and the fur trade. It was part civilized, part wild, part self-governing and part under the direct rule of the HBC. It was a colony whose inner tensions found release in the vastness of the country or were subdued by the necessity of co-operation. The Metis and most of the Indians were Catholic. Selkirk had provided the Catholics with 10,000 acres opposite the mouth of the Assiniboine River. There in 1818 Father Provencher celebrated a mass in the newly-built chapel dedicated to the patron saint of Selkirk's German-Catholic soldiers, St. Boniface. Thirty years later Provencher was Bishop of St. Boniface, presiding over a religious, medical, and educational establishment spread along the banks of the Red River to include St. Charles, St. Norbert, St. Paul, Ste. Agathe, and then west along the Assiniboine to St. Francois Xavier.

Many HBC men chose to retire in Red River with their Indian wives and half-breed children. They were often better educated, wealthier, and more cultivated than the other inhabitants of the colony, and they added an element of sophistication that was much appreciated. They were a constantly growing faction, and the increase in their numbers was reflected in the growth of the Anglican Church. Its parishes ran north along the west bank of the Red to St. John's, St. Andrew, St. Paul's (Middlechurch), St. Peter's, and along the Assiniboine to St. James and Headingly, Poplar Point, and Portage la Prairie. By 1849 Red River was the centre of the Diocese of Rupert's Land, with educational facilities which eventually became St. John's College. The Gaelic-speaking Presbyterian Sutherland Scots were centred in Kildonan, named for their home in Scotland. The Methodists were strong in the north, where James Evans devised the Cree alphabet so the Indians could learn to read and write.

For several decades this inland colony grew in its isolation, self-sufficient in food, exporting furs, and importing all manner of goods through the HBC. But as the Americans spread over the continent, isolation, and with it the power of the HBC, began to wane. By the 1830s increasing numbers of Metis were slipping across the American border to trade for cheaper and more varied goods. The HBC made strenuous efforts to enforce its monopoly through the government and the courts, both of which it controlled. Tension mounted between the people and the company but, as was so often the case in British North America, the problem was resolved by the courts rather than violence. In 1849 the HBC accused a Métis hunter, Guillaume Sayer, of illegal trading. Three hundred armed Métis led by Jean Louis Riel (father of Louis Riel) surrounded the courthouse. Sayer was found guilty, but the jury recommended clemency and the wise judge discharged him. It was a test case: the HBC monopoly was over. The winds of change had begun to stir. The 1850s would be the last quiet decade in the Canadian West.

From British to Canadian Colony
1850—1870

By mid-century isolation was ending. Trade with the United States was expanding. In 1859 the first steam boat appeared on the Red River linking the colony to Minnesota. The Age of Railways began to change the West profoundly as, in 1859, the HBC began to import goods by American railways instead of through the Bay. The same year saw the birth of the first newspaper in Winnipeg, the Nor'Wester, soon to be edited by John Schultz, a member of the increasingly large and vocal faction from Central Canada. Immigration from the Canadas and the United States was quickening, and with it the conflicting pressures for closer ties to Upper Canada or to Minnesota. Unfortunately for Manitoba, the Ontario immigrants brought with them a host of religious and racial animosities which were soon to cause trouble. Perhaps the clearest indication of change was the widespread belief that the charter of the HBC would not be renewed when it expired in 1859. In Red River itself the company was increasingly unable to exercise control, and becoming less willing to assume the burden of government when it had lost it monopoly and the fur trade was in decline. But it would fight to maintain the charter either for its own sake or to maximize compensation for its loss.

To the south the vibrant American Republic was stretching ever westward and northward, and if it could conquer Texas from Mexico and wrest Oregon from Britain, perhaps it could grasp the whole of the north-west quarter of the continent. "Manifest Destiny", the curious American belief that the entire continent was theirs, had been checked in the war of 1812-14—perhaps now it could outflank the Canadas on the west. Minnesotans certainly regarded the whole Red River valley as their patrimony. In the Canadas the West was coming to be viewed as the solution to a multitude of problems, including economic stagnation, the loss of free trade with the United States, and that eternal Canadian problem, constitutional crisis. Upper Canada was rapidly approaching the limits of good agricultural land, and it eagerly desired western expansion. Britain, in an anti-imperial and anti-monopoly mood, sought escape at minimum expense and bother from the demands of its troublesome colony and from the pressures on its North American empire of the United States in the south, of Russia in the north, and of both on the Pacific. At the same time, and in spite of all the efforts of the HBC to prove the contrary, a growing number of experts argued that the prairies were suitable for settlement and could sustain a large population. The only real question was whether that population would be Canadian or American—there were no alternatives.

Canada wanted Rupert's Land, Britain preferred Canadian ownership to American or Russian, and the HBC, ever realistic, wanted the maximum price for its withdrawal. In London, the House of Commons decided in 1859 to renew HBC control of the northern region, but left the way open for Canada to acquire the prairies. This could not occur until Upper and Lower Canada resolved their constitutional problems. In the meantime, Canada, assuming possession a foregone conclusion, sent explorers, settlers, and even surveyors to map out its empire beyond the St. Lawrence. With the constitutional crisis temporarily resolved by Confederation in 1867, serious negotiations began between the HBC and Canada.

While this was happening the situation at Red River was becoming increasingly confused. Though Canada was clearly destined to take over, the HBC government lingered on, a regime for which neither the geographical nor the jurisdictional limits had ever been clearly determined. Its power was rapidly waning, but no new authority emerged to fill the vacuum. The colony began to disintegrate into anarchy, a situation revealed quite clearly when the area around Portage la Prairie was declared Caledonia or Manitobah, with Thomas Spence as its first President. His government collapsed when the British Government refused to recognize it and one citizen refused to pay taxes.

Transfer of title from HBC to Canada should have been quite simple. In fact, the negotiation was quite bitter, and the outcome a near-tragedy for Manitoba and for Canada. Canada believed the land was British, so that all that was necessary was for Britain to transfer the title. It wanted everything for nothing. The HBC, on the other hand, thought it should be compensated in full for the loss of land it had never bought. The real sovereign, the British Government, abrogated responsibility throughout the negotiations, but finally agreed that the HBC should be compensated. In the final terms, Canada would pay the HBC £300,000 and the HBC would retain land around its posts and one-twentieth of the fertile land in the West, land it had recently declared to be useless.

In its haste the Canadian Government ignored the fact that ten thousand people already lived in the Red River colony. While rumours circulated of negotiations in Ottawa and in London, these people had never been informed of the developments that would so profoundly affect their lives. The rule of the HBC was clearly coming to an end, but no one told the inhabitants how or by what it would be replaced, or what the consequences would be for them. The HBC, inexplicably, sent neither information nor instructions to its Governor in Fort Garry. A certain nervousness was inevitable. That nervousness came to centre on one of the most important issues for a people in the midst of revolutionary change—the ownership of land. Many of the people had the title to the land that Selkirk had granted. But others had dubious titles, squatters' rights, or had never thought such things necessary since no Metis would take land occupied by another. They began to worry, as did the ones with legal titles when irresponsible members of the Canadian faction such as John Schultz deliberately spread rumours that HBC and Selkirk titles were invalid. People began to believe that the Canadians would seize all their land.

Rather than reassure these settlers by guaranteeing titles in this tiny fraction of the land Canada had just purchased, the Canadian Government perpetrated the one act most likely to exacerbate feelings. Before assuming the title from the HBC, before informing the inhabitants of what was happening, and without even informing the local authorities, Canada sent surveyors to stake out the land, and to do so in squares which totally violated the riverfront strips that had been occupied for generations. This survey halted abruptly when a young Métis with eighteen supporters stood on the survey chain and told the crew they had no right to survey land without the permission of the people who lived on it. The young man was Louis Riel. The struggle for the rights of the inhabitants, for provincial status, and for equality with the Eastern provinces had begun.

Failure to consult or even inform had provoked a crisis which was soon to deepen into rebellion. Was Ottawa aware of the situation? In the summer of 1869 the Governor of Red River, William McTavish, journeyed to Ottawa to offer advice; no one would listen to his warnings.

That same summer Bishop Taché of St. Boniface went to Ottawa attempting to obtain guarantees for the French language and Catholic rights; his request was ignored. Joseph Howe, a Cabinet Minister and champion of Nova Scotian rights, was in Manitoba that October to reassure the people, but there is no evidence that the Federal Government listened to whatever opinions he brought back from the West. The chief of the survey party conveyed his apprehensions to the Minister of Public Works; there was no answer.

From the moment he stopped the survey, Riel was the leader of the Métis, the largest group at Red River. Son of a literate miller, he had been born in St. Boniface twenty-five years earlier and educated in Montreal. Riel's character was the key to all he did. His brilliance, eloquence, concern for his people, and obvious leadership qualities were unfortunately marred by moodiness, authoritarianism, ill-temper, resentment of authority, overconfidence, and eventually the conviction that he had been called upon by God to protect the freedom of the Métis. Later that fervour became madness, but in 1869 Riel was one of the few who clearly understood what was happening.

Riel and the Métis accepted that Canada would acquire Rupert's Land. What they wanted was not to stop the transfer, but to have some say in the terms under which they became Canadian plus some protection of their rights. And, by a series of mistakes, Ottawa, London, and the HBC gave them the opportunity, for in 1869 there was no effective government at Red River. To fill the vacuum, Riel and the people organized a Provisional Government. One of its first acts was to stop at the American border the Lieutenant-Governor-elect, William McDougall. He had been the Minister of Public Works who had appointed a survey party and refused to listen to warnings of the unease a survey would provoke. Upon hearing that he had been stopped, the Canadian Government refused to pay the HBC until it and the British Government restored order. This the HBC was incapable of doing, and the British Government refused on the grounds that it was not responsible for the trouble. McDougall issued two proclamations from North Dakota, the first declaring, incorrectly, that title had been transferred, the second calling for the raising of troops. The latter was repudiated by Ottawa and McDougall ordered to say no more. The threat of troops and the further confusion over the title only served to increase anxiety in the colony.

Meanwhile, after seizing Fort Garry, Riel called for the election of an Assembly consisting of twelve English and twelve French delegates. No agreement emerged from this Assembly, but a second Assembly drafted a list of terms for joining Canada. They included title to land, protection of customs, territorial government to be followed by provincial status, control of public lands, better communications with Central Canada, and money for public works. The Assembly established a new Provisional Government, still consisting of twelve English-speaking and twelve French-speaking delegates. Although this government was technically illegal, Governor McTavish of the HBC recognized it. Riel was elected President, and three delegates, one English, one French, and one American, were elected to negotiate with Ottawa. This government also decided to free a group of Canadians who had been imprisoned in Fort Garry after organizing resistance to the first Provisional Government.

Suddenly the scene was darkened by a revolt against the new government. The Canadian faction had never accepted the domination of the colony by Riel and the Métis majority, an opposition that was based on a combination of self-interest and prejudice. Their hostility to Riel was encouraged by Thomas Scott, a bigoted Ontario Orangeman who had earlier escaped from Fort Garry. He, John Schultz, and Charles Boulton organized a group of Canadians in Portage la Prairie to march on Fort Garry and liberate the prisoners. This revolt petered out because Riel had freed most of these prisoners, because the Protestant clergy opposed an uprising, and because the great majority of the people supported Riel. Unfortunately, Schultz's men had captured a Métis, Norbert Parisien. While escaping from them Parisien shot and killed a Canadian, the first blood spilled in the whole affair. Parisien was recaptured and beaten to death, the first deliberate killing. The Portage group was captured in Winnipeg. Boulton was sentenced to death for treason, then reprieved by Riel. Scott was not so lucky. He was a firebrand in the Canadian cause, violent in temper and vicious in his attacks on Riel and the Métis both before and after his capture. Under the rules of the Métis hunt he was tried by jury for insubordination, found guilty, sentenced to death, and shot by the walls of Fort Garry.

In Manitoba the execution created little excitement. There was no more opposition to the Provisional Government, no more threat of civil war, and a tranquility settled over the colony for the first time in months. The divide-and-rule tactics of the Canadian Government and the Canadian faction ceased and the colony achieved sufficient cohesion to negotiate with Ottawa. In Ontario, on the other hand, the execution of an Orangeman by a Catholic Métis court provoked a violent backlash. Demands for revenge and the suppression of Red River by force were made, even though Red River was not yet part of Canada. The country became seriously divided on racial and religious lines, severely restricting Prime Minister John A. Macdonald's capacity to deal with the situation.

Provincial Status
1870

While the Orange Order, in the aftermath of Scott's execution, was fanning the flames of bigotry in Ontario, the three delegates from Manitoba were on their way to Ottawa to negotiate the terms under which the inhabitants of Red River would enter the Canadian Confederation. Their instructions had been drafted mainly by Riel who, on his own authority and in contradiction to the specific instructions of the Convention, insisted on immediate provincial status. With it, Riel hoped, Manitoba rather than some distant and unsympathetic government would control religion, education, and land. A second point Riel insisted upon was that the Metis be given specific land grants. More conditions were added by Bishop Tache and others: Manitoba should have a constitution like that of Quebec, a parochial school system, and a bicameral legislature.

On their arrival in Ottawa in March 1870, two of the delegates were arrested for the murder of Scott. This was hardly an auspicious manner in which to begin negotiations, but the two were soon released and talks began. Having conceded Riel's main point—that Manitoba should negotiate its entry into Confederation—John A. Macdonald and his Quebec lieutenant George Etienne Cartier quickly settled the details, the negotiations lasting less than a week. Canada's concessions were considerable. Red River was granted provincial status, something Ottawa had never dreamed of doing in 1869. Riel became the Father of Manitoba, the man who led the fifth province into Confederation and, hence, a Father of Confederation. Like the other Fathers of Confederation, he fought for what he believed was necessary for his province, and like the other Fathers he compromised many of his demands in the interests of the broader Confederation. At Riel's insistence the province was called Manitoba. The form of government was that requested by Tache, a bicameral legislature and a Lieutenant-Governor appointed by Ottawa—just like the other provinces. The province obtained two Senators and four seats in the federal House of Commons. Metis and other claims to land were to be recognized, something which, if done in 1869, might have averted the crisis. The Metis were also given land west of Red River. Manitoba obtained control of education as Riel and Tache had demanded. This ensured equal rights for Protestant and Catholic, with toleration for all and domination by none—just, fair, equitable. By this method minority rights were preserved, and the minority in 1870 was English and Protestant.

In turn Manitoba made, or was forced to accept, a number of major concessions. First, the area of the new province was limited to the small rectangle of land around Winnipeg. It became known as the postage-stamp province, for it extended only from Beausejour on the east to just west of Portage la Prairie, and from the American border to Lake Winnipeg. It was less than one hundred miles on each side, approximately four per-cent of the present Manitoba or one-third of the area of New Brunswick at the time. Canada had conceded to Manitoba less than one per-cent of Rupert's Land. The boundaries question soon became a major problem in federal-provincial relations, and was not resolved until 1912.

The second Manitoban concession was more serious. While granting provincial status, Ottawa retained control of Crown lands, that is, of all natural resources, be they agricultural land, mineral wealth, forest, or river. The original four provinces retained control of their natural resources when they entered Confederation, as did Prince Edward Island and British Columbia which entered after Manitoba. Only Manitoba, and later Saskatchewan and Alberta, were denied control of their own natural resources. This made Manitoba a second-class province. It introduced from the beginning of Confederation the concept of two classes of provinces: the eastern ones and British Columbia which controlled their resources for the benefit of their own people and the prairie provinces whose resources were controlled by Ottawa for the benefit of the entire country. It was an act of discrimination which created an attitude of distrust toward Central Canada and the central government which has never died, possibly because the idea has persisted in parts of Canada that the resources of the prairies should be treated differently from those of the other provinces.

The federal government argued that it had to control Manitoban land in order to populate the West and build a transcontinental railway. This was questionable. Manitoba would soon be as dedicated to the settlement of the West as the federal government. No province needed a transcontinental railway more than Manitoba, which was completely land-locked and isolated. The Canadian Pacific Railway (CPR) was built for more than a thousand miles through provinces where the federal government did not control natural resources; the same could have been easily done in Manitoba. The province was only one-hundred miles wide, perhaps one-seventh the distance across the prairies, and the federal government had complete control of the rest of Rupert's Land with millions of acres of land to sell or give away. Finally, in return for control of natural resources, Manitoba would willingly have given the federal government sufficient unsettled land to support railway construction. In short, the federal government bought Rupert's Land in order to have a Canadian colony. Although forced by Riel to grant provincial status to a tiny fraction of it, Ottawa had no intention of relinquishing economic control over any of it.

The third failure of the negotiators was in obtaining a meaningful amnesty for the men who had participated in the Rebellion. In December 1869 the Governor of Canada issued an amnesty providing the Métis laid down their weapons. This amnesty was never proclaimed in Red River. In 1870 Bishop Taché of St. Boniface received assurances from Ottawa that this amnesty was both valid and comprehensive. Father N.J. Ritchot, one of the negotiators, received similar assurances from George Cartier, however the latter also said that amnesty might be a matter for the British Government, and he put nothing in writing.

Worried by this ambiguity, Bishop Taché journeyed to Ottawa in the summer of 1870. He received further verbal assurances from Cartier and, on that basis, assured Riel that a full amnesty had been granted. The promise of amnesty was broken. In 1874 Ambroise Lepine, President of the court that had tried Scott, was arrested, tried, and found guilty of murder. The Governor-General commuted the sentence to two years in prison. The Canadian Government then granted a full amnesty to all participants except Riel, Lepine, and W.B. O'Donoghue, who received partial amnesties conditional upon several years' banishment. Lepine's trial and the broken promise infuriated French Catholics and the Métis; failure to hang Riel and punish his followers infuriated the English and the Protestants. The unfortunate mishandling of this issue exacerbated divisions during the vital first years of the province.

The same harmful effects resulted from the arrival of the Wolseley expedition. Peace reigned in Red River in the spring of 1870. The Rebellion was over; Manitoba was a province; the people had received the guarantees of rights and title to land for which they had been forced to rebel. For them the crisis had ended. But for Central Canada the Riel Rebellion was far from over. Before the Manitoban negotiators ever arrived in Ottawa, and before Ottawa even acquired title to Rupert's Land, the federal government was raising one thousand troops at great expense to occupy by force what it had purchased on credit. The alleged reason for the expedition was to restore order. Yet that spring there was no disorder in Red River. The expedition was really dispatched to mollify public opinion in Ontario, to occupy the colony militarily, to punish Riel and his supporters, and to show the flag to the Indians and the Americans.

The troops were quickly mobilized and sent west under Colonel Ernest Wolseley. The soldiers were mainly Orange Protestant volunteers, and in fact the Manitoba chapter of the Orange Lodge was organized en route. As they approached Red River there was growing apprehension that they were bent on revenge for Scott's execution. As this fear grew it reinforced, and in turn was reinforced by, the ambiguities in Ottawa's statements about an amnesty. Upon arrival the troops were drawn up in battle formation to advance on the undefended and open-gated Fort Garry, where some nervous members of the Provisional Government awaited them.

Riel fled moments before troops arrived, without a warrant, to arrest him. Others were not so lucky. The ill-disciplined soldiers took the law into their own hands. Andre Nault, on whose land the survey party had been stopped, was beaten half to death. Elzear Goulet, one of Scott's jurors, drowned trying to escape from a mob. Other acts of vigilante justice were perpetrated as the soldiers did more damage in nine days than had occurred under nine months of Riel's Provisional Government. Several days later the new Lieutenant-Governor arrived to take possession of the territory from the Governor of the HBC. Thus did the Red River Rebellion end; thus did Manitoba become a province.

Uncertain Development
1870—1880

Manitoba was the only part of Canada to attain provincial status before it acquired responsible government. Under this unique British institution the people vote for political parties which then obtain seats in the Legislative Assembly, the leaders of the dominant group forming the Government or Cabinet. The latter is directly responsible to the Assembly, and if it loses the confidence of a majority in that Assembly, must resign and be replaced or call an election. Responsible government was achieved by popular pressure and rebellion in the Maritimes and the Canadas before Confederation. In Manitoba it was created by a federally-appointed Lieutenant-Governor.

To a certain extent provincial status was precipitate. The population was small, heterogeneous, and without democratic traditions or experience. The one group that had democratic experience, the Ontario-British minority, had an undemocratic contempt for the rights of the Métis, Indian, and Catholic majority. The latter were a shrinking majority, unsure of how to guarantee their rights. There was no basic agreement on the type of society Manitoba should become. To grant provincial status to a society in flux was risky. In addition, the area was too small to be a viable province, transportation was quite inadequate, and there were few imports to sustain customs revenue. For years much of the revenue and government personnel had to be supplied from Ottawa as the young province struggled to attain stability, growth, and maturity.

At first all aspects of government were dominated by Lieutenant-Governor Adams Archibald. He organized the first government, applied existing laws and proclaimed new ones. A census identified a population of 12,000, more than half Catholic, containing 5,700 Métis, 4,000 English half-breeds, and 1,500 whites, half of whom had been born in the colony. Twelve English and twelve French constituencies were mapped out, and the government party, which Archibald had organized, won twenty of the twenty-four seats. This Assembly quickly produced a mixed constitution with British courts, Ontario laws, and the Quebec school system. Archibald and his successor, Alexander Morris, dominated the Cabinet and drafted most of its laws. But within a few years Morris turned the direction of affairs over to a premier. Responsible government was working. The two-party system took longer to develop, but by 1890 the Government could be identified as Liberal, the Opposition as Conservative, and party lines had definitely been drawn.

Agriculture developed slowly, the first exports of wheat taking place in 1876. The replacement of millstones by steel rollers in the milling industry made possible the use of hard wheat, the type best suited to the prairies. Manitoba Number 1 Hard became an international standard for grading wheat. Red Fife wheat, which required ten to twenty days less to mature, became the first grain really suited to the short growing season of the West. The movement of wheat was vastly improved when it was realized that bulk wheat could be treated as a liquid rather than a solid, and poured from waggon to elevator to box car instead of being carried in bags as had been done for centuries.

As the pace of economy quickened, Winnipeg grew into the transportation and business centre of the West, its population jumping from three hundred in 1870 to over five thousand by 1875. After a recession in the late 1870s, a boom struck Winnipeg in 1880, with real estate prices tripling and lots selling in the suburbs where building did not actually occur for decades. The boom was fuelled by wild speculation and a mindless faith in the future. It collapsed within the year. Real economic progress would have to await the pull of the world economic resurgence that was to begin in 1896. Yet the collapse of the boom and the subsequent pessimism masked real growth. The CPR spent massively on a station, sheds, and roundhouses. A bewildering array of hotels, warehouses, stores, mills, banks, small factories, machine shops, government buildings, and houses were thrown up. Though the boom had collapsed, Winnipeg's population doubled between 1880 and 1885.

At first the settlers in the new Manitoba insisted on two geographic features in addition to good land—access to water for transportation and to wood for fuel and shelter. As these features are rare on the prairies, the first patterns of settlement were sharply restricted, simply extending existing communities. Gradually, the settlers spread out from the Red and Assiniboine and other rivers, moving farther and farther back from the river banks. Such names as Springfield, Stoney Mountain, Emerson, and Morris appeared on the map.

The first settlers to move into the open plain were the German-speaking Mennonites. Interpreting literally the commandment "Thou shall not kill", they had always refused military service and had hence become the object of persecution by European governments and societies. After obtaining exemption from military service plus guarantees of freedom of religion, they came to Manitoba in the thousands in the 1870s, peopling the area around Steinbach, Altona, and Morden. Coming from a similar geography and climate in Russia, they were the first settlers to know how to farm the dry prairies. This knowledge, combined with their habits of hard work, frugality, innovation, and community co-operation, quickly produced success and later prosperity. They have been one of the pillars of Manitoban society ever since.

Icelanders began arriving in the mid-1870s, settling an area similar to the one they had left, on the west shore of Lake Winnipeg around a town they named Gimli, or "Paradise", and in an area they called New Iceland. The topography they chose was one of mixed pastureland, bush, and farmland where they could combine fishing, farming, and hunting. In spite of early difficulties, these remarkably hardy and self-sufficient people prospered and integrated themselves quickly into the increasingly complex cultural mosaic that was Manitoba.

The French Canadians formed another major source of immigration in this period. Quebec, which had almost reached the limits of good agricultural land, witnessed its surplus population spilling over into Ontario and New England where language and culture were endangered. This was one of the reasons some Quebec politicians supported the Confederation, for they saw the West as a potential homeland for their own people. French Canadians began migrating to the West, expanding the existing French settlement on the east bank of the Red, forming pockets of settlement throughout the province but concentrating around St. Boniface. By all appearances they were not as wealthy, well educated, ambitious, organized, or aggressive as the Protestant emigrants from Ontario. Certainly they fought a strong rearguard action to preserve their rights, but they have never wielded an influence in Manitoba in proportion to their numbers.

In contrast, a tiny minority which has always made a contribution and wielded an influence out of all proportion to its size is the Jewish community. Coming largely from Russia, they quickly established themselves in the shops, small industries such as textiles, and eventually in law, commerce, and medicine. They soon adapted to democratic politics, supporting and influencing most political parties. Their contribution to the arts, education, and culture has been outstanding.

The dominant group, though, came from English-speaking, Protestant Ontario. Though described as Anglo-Saxons, many were Scottish, Irish, or Anglo-Irish, with Presbyterians outnumbering Anglicans. In Ontario, settlement was reaching the border of agricultural land, one of the reasons Canada had acquired Rupert's Land. Ontarians were drifting into the Red River area in the 1860s, and this migration accelerated after Manitoba became a province. Nevertheless, in the 1870s Protestants gradually came to outnumber Catholics, whites replaced Métis and half-breeds as the numerical majority, English replaced French as the dominant language, and the easy-going ways of the buffalo hunt gave way to the Protestant work ethic and a rather narrow, intolerant puritanism which developed, paradoxically, side-by-side with the roaring, drunken frontier town that was Winnipeg. The Ontario-British settled the good land in the south-west of the province, particularly after Indian rights had been extinguished by treaties in the early 1870s. They were experienced farmers, had capital and equipment, and were well educated and extremely self-confident. They soon came to dominate the province politically, economically, and socially. It was a domination that would last, some would say, until the victory of the New Democratic Party in 1969. Others would argue that their domination of the province has never ended.

Much of this wave of settlement accompanied the building of the CPR. Thinking it would become the transportation and commercial centre of western Manitoba, a small village named itself Rapid City. But the railway passed elsewhere, Rapid City remained a village, and it was Brandon, instead, which grew from nothing to a population of two thousand between 1880 and 1882. A railway crew can work roughly four miles out in each direction from its base, so there are towns or villages located every eight miles along the track, more important ones at sixteen or thirty-two miles, and main centres approximately every one hundred fifty miles. The CPR spawned a string of such towns across southern Manitoba at sixteen-mile intervals—Carberry, Brandon, Oak Lake, Virden, Elkhorn. Each town looks roughly the same, with elevators, loading platforms, and coal and lumber sheds on one side of the tracks, main street and the residential area on the other. The school is several blocks back from the tracks so the trains would neither endanger nor disturb the pupils, and the fairgrounds and stockyards are at the extremities of the little hamlets. Often these towns conform to the square-mile survey system, with eighteen blocks to the mile, the streets sometimes unimaginatively named First, Second, Third going west and, for symmetry, First Street East in the opposite direction.

As settlement spread north and south of the main line these towns boomed and were incorporated. Farmers had to come to them from as far as fifty miles. Some of them were larger in the 1880s than they are today, and they often boasted several hotels to entertain the farmers, who might have to wait more than a day to unload a waggonload of wheat. Later on, to the south, another string of towns edged westward along a branch line—Crystal City, Killarney, Deloraine, Boissevain, Souris, Melita. To the north there developed a parallel line of towns—Gladstone, Neepawa, Minnedosa, Birtle, Russell. Much of this settlement was British, but a few Scandinavians inhabited the slopes of Riding Mountain. By the mid-1890s much of the agricultural land of Manitoba was filled in, though pockets remained and later waves of immigration would push into the Dauphin plain and the forest belt to the north of the plains.

With the prairie sod rapidly yielding to the advance of settlement, the postage-stamp province chafed in the straitjacket of the borders it had been given in 1870. It yearned to expand to the east, west, and north and if not to acquire equality with Ontario and Quebec, at least to achieve parity with Nova Scotia and New Brunswick. To the east the border with Ontario had never been settled. That required a showdown known as the Battle of Rat Portage (Kenora). Manitoba wanted the border fixed at the western tip of Lake Superior; Ontario wanted it at the western tip of Lake of the Woods. Both provinces established newspapers in the disputed area, both sent police forces, and both licensed liquor outlets to serve the railway construction crews. Each police force arrested the salesmen licensed by the opposite government, leaving the market to the bootleggers. Ontario created the electoral seat of Rat Portage; Manitoba did the same. Ontario called an election; Manitoba did the same. On the same day the area sent deputies to both Toronto and Winnipeg.

The federal government of Sir John A. Macdonald agreed with Manitoba that the border should be drawn near Thunder Bay. It had the legal power to determine new provincial borders, as it had already done in Manitoba and was to do for Alberta and Saskatchewan. Much of the disputed land was, in fact, federal land purchased from the HBC in 1869. Nevertheless, its electoral strength rested in Ontario, not Manitoba, and it would have been political folly to support the province with the fewest votes against the province with the most.

Instead of making a decision, the federal government referred the matter to the British Privy Council in 1884. Ontario could and did hire the best lawyers available; Manitoba could not. The Privy Council handed down their verdict in Ontario's favour, rejecting even the compromise of the watershed between Lakes Superior and Winnipeg. The border was fixed at Lake of the Woods, less than one hundred miles from Winnipeg, more than one thousand from Toronto. Manitoba had lost its eastern hinterland and a wealth of timber and mineral resources.

More significantly, by not extending the western border to the Rockies at that time, the federal government had virtually ensured that the prairies would not become a single province, despite the large degree of economic, geographic, and ethnic similarity. The federal government wanted to retain complete control of the development of this area, and the decision to limit Manitoba's western border paved the way for the separate political development of the three provinces. The prairies would be permanently weakened within the federal system by having three provincial governments instead of one. With the regions of Ontario and Quebec under single governments and the West divided into four, Canadians had created an unbalanced federal system that has never worked smoothly.

Railways, Schools,
and Provincial Rights
1880—1896

With provincial status, the westward migration of the Métis, the settlement of Indian claims, the establishment of stable government, larger
borders, and with settlers gradually opening up the prairies to agricultural production, only one major handicap seemed to stand between
Manitoba and an unlimited future—adequate railway facilities. Without
an extensive network of railways plus access to international markets,
the Manitoban economy simply could not develop. A railway link to
the outside world was finally forged in 1878 when the first train chugged
into St. Boniface from St. Paul, Minnesota. The hoot of the steam
locomotive was to be one of the most familiar sounds on the prairies
for the next seventy years.

Then optimism exploded when the CPR, staggering ever westward
over a trail of muskeg, rock, politics, and corruption, approached the
province in 1882. As it did, a major debate erupted as to where it
would cross the Red River. The CPR bridgehead on the Red, as the
junction of the east-west transcontinental and the existing north-south
settlement pattern and transportation system, would be the major
prairie metropolis for decades to come. Here the CPR would establish
its facilities to service the entire transportation network of the prairies.
Here would be built the warehouses for the distribution of goods going
west and the elevators, stock yards, and meat-packing plants for exports
to the east. There were two possible sites: Winnipeg, where the existing
population was concentrated, and Selkirk, where the Red did not flood
and could be easily bridged. The CPR surveyors strongly recommended
Selkirk, citing the enormity of the floods that frequently inundated

Winnipeg. But Winnipeg offered a free bridge, free land for the railway yards, and exemption from property taxes forever. The CPR opted for eternal tax exemption despite the excessive construction costs of crossing the Red at the wrong geographic place. It was a victory for the Winnipeg merchants, but an expensive mistake for Manitoba. By unnecessarily bribing the CPR to cross at Winnipeg, Manitobans forfeited hundreds of millions of dollars in tax revenue, doomed the city and the province to hundreds of millions of dollars of flood damage, and destined a goodly portion of the province's population to the annual threat and the all-too-frequent reality of flood.

The railway brought a short-lived boom, but not the sustained economic development envisaged. In fact, hope soon gave way to despair. A bitterness and frustration with the railways and the federal government emerged which, never far from the surface in Western Canada, overflows with each downturn in economic fortunes. The tie that was to bind Confederation and the federal government's National Policy was the CPR. It would stretch from coast to coast—good politics, but economic nonsense as there was no real market west of southern Ontario. Until a Western market emerged, the government and the railway would face enormous debts resulting from the heavy costs of construction. The bulk of Canada's population, wealth, production, and freight was concentrated in Central Canada, and Macdonald taxed it as much as was politically feasible. But the government and the CPR could not tax that existing traffic enough to pay for the westward expansion, as there were already competing railway and steamship systems in Central Canada and the people were politically powerful. The new parts of the line were being built in the west, so the CPR was given a monopoly there, the area with least population, the greatest distances, and no alternative method of transportation. Thus, for goods being exported, Westerners would obtain the world price minus whatever shipping rate the CPR charged, and that included goods sold to the rest of Canada. The freight rates from Manitoba to Fort William became the largest single expense of Manitoba farmers. For imported goods, Westerners would pay the Central Canadian tariff-protected price plus whatever transportation rate the CPR charged. The benefits of the CPR flowed to all Canadians, but the costs were born disproportionately by the West.

At first Manitoba did not object to the CPR monopoly. One railway would have been sufficient—if it had built the branch lines so desperately needed and charged a fair rate. Yet the CPR refused to build branch lines; as the only line in the West, the farmers had to come to it, even if the distance were fifty miles and took several days. Not only that, but

as the only railway, it could charge what it wanted, and did so. In the 1880s railways became the most important, and nearly the only issue in Manitoban politics, as the government and people desperately sought escape from economic strangulation.

The government of Premier John Norquay attempted to charter railways to link up with American lines, in the hope that this would initiate competition. The federal government immediately disallowed the charters. The Opposition in the Manitoba Assembly promised a tougher policy, and Norquay's support fell to twenty-one out of thirty-five seats in the 1886 election. In a bid to regain support, Norquay chartered the Red River Valley Railway (RRVR) to run to the United States. The federal government disallowed it within a month. The Winnipeg Board of Trade suggested that the West should separate if Ottawa did not yield on the issue. Norquay then passed a bill to build the line as a public work, something within provincial jurisdiction. The CPR hastily threw a line in front of the intended route of the RRVR so that Ottawa could grant a court injunction preventing the RRVR from crossing CPR land. Nonetheless, Norquay promised to build the line "unless prevented from doing so by legal or military force".

He should have added political deceit, for he clearly under-estimated the determination of Sir John A. Macdonald, who, of course, was concerned with the overall problem of nation-building and not the economic grievances of a small group of prairie farmers. Manitoba had constructed forty miles of line toward Hudson Bay for which, under the policy whereby the federal government granted land to all railway builders, the province was owed 256,000 acres. Macdonald promised the Provincial Treasurer that the land would be transferred. With this land as collateral Norquay issued bonds to pay for the construction of the RRVR. Macdonald refused to yield the land and denied he had ever said he would transfer it. The bonds thus stood without collateral, and Norquay and the Treasurer were forced to resign. He had failed; his government was defeated.

By this time Macdonald was beginning to realize that the prolonged battle with Manitoba was becoming politically expensive and that a compromise must be reached. Such a compromise was settled with the new Liberal Premier of Manitoba, Thomas Greenway, who was as determined as Norquay to obtain railway competition. For $15,000,000 the federal government bought out the monopoly clause in the CPR charter. One major obstacle had been removed, but was it enough? Greenway immediately began building railways to compete with the CPR. Infuriated, the CPR tried blackmail: unless the Manitoba Govern-

ment leased the RRVR to the CPR, the CPR would not build any branches south of the main line. Greenway rejected the threat, called an election, and won thirty-three out of thirty-eight seats. Thus confirmed in his course of action, he negotiated the creation of the ambitiously-named Northern Pacific and Manitoba Railway (NP&MR), which was to take over the RRVR and build a line from Morris to Souris. One of their lines had to cross an existing CPR line at Fort Whyte, which it did—at night. The next day the CPR sent a crew to tear up the crossing. The Manitoba Government sent three hundred constables to "prevent disorder", that is, to ensure a victory for Manitoba. As is usual in Canada, the matter went to the courts. They decided in Manitoba's favour. Like the HBC monopoly a generation earlier, the CPR monopoly had ended, politically, legally, and in fact.

Manitoba had apparently won, but it was a hollow victory. While it is true that one company is a monopoly, it does not necessarily follow that two companies create competition. The CPR and the NP&MR quickly came to terms, divided the traffic between themselves, and maintained the rates at the CPR's level. Manitoba did obtain additional lines, but Greenway had essentially failed to solve the problems of transportation. Manitobans were doubly angry because to support the NP&MR, Greenway had sacrificed the proposed railway to Hudson Bay. Under provincial control this railway might have provided both competition and direct access to world trade. By the late 1880s Greenway was in serious political trouble, but he found salvation in religion; that is, in the politics of religion.

As railways, villages, and farmhouses spread across the plains, so did the network of little schoolhouses. The development of education quickly led to political trouble. The Manitoban education system had, at the founding of the province, been based on the parochial principle. Protestant and Catholic communities had their own systems, each supported from taxes that were divided on a per capita basis. Although Catholics were in a majority, with separate schools neither group would dominate, dictate to, nor inflict its peculiar bias on the other. The system was equitable, just, tolerant, and designed to minimize conflict. Three factors conspired to destroy this ideal balance. Immigration to the province was overwhelmingly Protestant, and all too often tinged with an Orange intolerance for all things Catholic. Secondly, the developing racial and religious antagonisms in Central Canada were carried to Manitoba by the settlers. Finally, the Greenway Government was floundering, and the language and education issues could provide a means of masking the government's multiple failures.

In 1889 and 1890 Greenway swung into action. The use of French was abolished in the courts, legislature, and government documents. Catholic holidays ceased to be public holidays, and the right of a Frenchman to trial by a jury at least half French was abolished—trial by peers would tend to be trial by Protestants. All Catholic and Protestant school boards were abolished to be replaced by non-sectarian boards drawn from the general public. These boards, the new teachers, and the new curriculum were "non-religious", but they naturally reflected the cultural values of the majority of the people, and that majority was clearly Protestant. Bishop Taché had defended a system that had protected the English when they were the minority, but with the English as the majority, the rules of the game had changed. The Catholics challenged the new legislation in the courts. Local courts, with their Protestant majorities, supported the legislation; the issue was taken higher where the federal courts supported Catholic rights. The final court of appeal, the Privy Council in London, agreed with the provincial government because the new legislation did not deny the Catholics the right to operate their own schools—it just made them pay an additional tax to do so.

Noting the popularity of his actions, and basking in the glow of the favourable Privy Council decision, Greenway called an election. The populace, ignoring all other issues, gave him a clear majority. Having failed in the courts and in the election, the Catholics asked the federal government to protect the rights that were guaranteed when Manitoba joined Confederation. The federal Conservative Government was caught between the extremes of Protestant bigotry and Catholic minority rights. However reluctant, it had to act. The resulting clash was perhaps the greatest showdown in Canadian history between a provincial and the federal government. The federal government issued an Order-in-Council demanding that the Greenway Government give the Catholic schools a portion of the education budget. Manitoba refused, arguing that education was a provincial matter. Greenway called another election to give himself a mandate to stand up to Ottawa. He won handsomely. The federal Conservatives, who had long since run out of ideas, ideals, policies, principles, and leaders, could not cope with the situation. They dithered, disintegrated, exhausted their five-year mandate, and were forced to call an election they could not win.

The newly-elected federal Liberal Government of Sir Wilfrid Laurier had no real policy on the Manitoba School Question. Given the magnitude of the Conservative failure, it did not need one. Laurier gave in to Protestant Manitoba, one of the paradoxes of Canadian politics, as the base of his support was Catholic Quebec. Manitoba yielded a few concessions—if there was a significant minority in a school, at least one teacher should come from that minority. But Manitoba had won and Ottawa had lost. Canadian Protestants cheered the Manitoban victory, yet one wonders what would have happened if Quebec had done to its English minority what Manitoba did to its French.

Promise Fulfilled
1896 — 1918

For twenty-five years the province had struggled unsuccessfully to achieve the promise many believed it to hold. Foundations had been laid, obstacles both natural and human had been conquered, but the anticipated waves of immigration had never come, and of those settlers who arrived, many wandered on to the United States. Suddenly in 1896 the tide turned. The discovery of vast quantities of gold in South Africa and the Yukon produced one of the greatest eras of prosperity in world history, lasting roughly from 1896 until 1913. Credit at low rates became available for railway, industrial, commercial, and residential construction. Wheat prices increased, and, what was more important and rare, they increased more rapidly than the price of manufactured goods. The development of Marquis wheat reduced the growing season by twenty days, and crop failures became more infrequent.

The European population explosion of the nineteenth century spilled over and a new and mighty wave of immigration swept over North America. This time much of it stayed in Canada, because the last American frontier had been reached. For the same reason thousands of Americans emigrated to Western Canada, and though they were quickly assimilated into the British population, their political ideas and cultural values became an extremely significant influence in the prairies. The wave of immigration filled the pockets of vacant land, occupied the area to the north and west of Dauphin, and added massive Slavic and American minorities to the already polyglot population. From 1891 to 1901 Manitoba's population jumped from 150,000 to 250,000, and stood at 550,000 by 1916. It has not even doubled since then.

With the world enjoying unprecedented prosperity and the prairies rapidly filling with eager immigrants, Winnipeg experienced tremendous growth. Its role as the major prairie metropolis gave it a profit on all economic activity in the West. It supplied many of the goods needed from its own rising industries—textiles, harness, farm implements, breweries, construction supplies, and every kind of machine good. What it did not manufacture it distributed, and enormous warehouses such as J. H. Ashdowns came to dominate Main Street between Portage Avenue and the CPR. Winnipeg became one of the greatest transportation centres in North America and a regional centre for three major railway systems, the CPR, the Grand Trunk Pacific, and the Canadian Northern, with acres of sidings, sheds, and shops. The wheat of the West flowed through its facilities, and its Grain Exchange helped to set world prices. Secondary agricultural industry such as meat processing became a major employer. The city was one of the financial centres of Canada, with branches of all major banks, trust and insurance companies, and stock and real estate brokers. With the population tripling between 1895 and 1907, hotel and residential construction could not keep pace with demand. Suburbs spread out along the street-car lines, the old slums along the CPR were replaced, and the wealthy built their mansions along Wellington Crescent. Government construction added to the boom: a Post Office, a Land Titles Office, an Agricultural School, the Medical School, Immigration Hall, Fort Osborne Barracks, and, of course, schools, libraries, and hospitals. One of the best indications of Winnipeg's boundless optimism was the solution to the problem of water supply. There were two alternatives: to develop some springs fifteen miles away for $2,000,000, which would be adequate for the immediate future, or to construct an aqueduct to Shoal Lake one hundred miles away for $14,000,000, which would ensure supply for generations. The city council recommended the former, but the citizens had a reckless optimistic view of their future. They rejected the council's proposal, and Winnipeg acquired a water supply that, today, serves a modern industrial city that has twice doubled in population.

Riding this new wave of prosperity and contributing vigorously to it was a new and energetic Conservative administration. Its rise to power was natural, for the Greenway Government had been too long in office, had failed to change Ottawa's tariff or railway policies, had failed to obtain better borders or control of natural resources, had lost its best lieutenants as governments are prone to do after a decade in power, and had long since milked the Manitoba School Question for all its political benefits. The new premier, Rodmond Roblin, was to govern the province from 1900 to 1915. His government developed one of the most success-ful and corrupt political machines in Canadian history. It was broadly based at first, including much of the Anglo-Saxon bloc plus a majority of the French and ethnic votes, which had been appeased with bilingual schools. It opposed prohibition, which gave it the financial support of the liquor interests plus the ethnic vote, though this was to eventually cost it much English support. The electorate, particularly the newly-arrived immigrant, was courted with bribery, liquor, minor government positions, government contracts, and, of course, jobs in highway and railway construction. Anglo-Saxons were distressed by the crassness of the purchase of the ethnic vote, but the foreigners eventually learned to play the political game. Within a generation hundreds of thousands of East Europeans who had never known democracy had been assimilated into the Canadian tradition. Their descendants have been stalwart supporters of democracy ever since.

Prosperity brought tax revenue, which was augmented by the first attempts in Canada to tax corporate wealth. Much of this revenue was invested in railways, still the greatest need of the province. Roblin leased the NP&MR to the Canadian Northern, and the latter constructed the largest network of lines in Manitoba, extended it to Lake Superior, reduced the rates by fifteen per-cent, and forced the CPR to offer fair freight rates. Just as the railways had been inadequate and expensive, so too was the service provided by Bell Telephone. It was operated as a profit-making monopoly, and so refused to extend lines into the thinly-populated parts of the province, precisely where they were most needed. In 1908 Bell was nationalized, and Manitoba became the first govern-ment in North America to operate a telephone company. Coverage was soon extended to rural areas, service was improved, and the rates were reduced, an excellent example of public enterprise.

Roblin never hesitated to intervene in the economy if he felt that private enterprise was failing to serve the interests of the people. When the Grain Exchange expelled the representative of the farmers' Grain Growers Grain Company, Roblin ordered him reinstated or he would force the issue by legislation. The government moved quickly into other areas where private companies proved inadequate, building, for example, the St. Boniface stockyards and meatpacking plant. In 1906 Winnipeg took over its own supply of electricity, damned the Winnipeg River, cut the price of hydro-electric power from twenty to three cents per kilowatt hour, and provided the cheapest power in North America for decades.

One of Roblin's greatest victories was the achievement of Manitoba's present boundaries. Even after the adjustment of 1881 Manitoba was still a tiny province. This grievance became unbearable when, in 1905, Saskatchewan and Alberta became provinces and received at the same time the 60th latitude as their northern border, thus extending over twice as far north as the oldest and proudest prairie province. Premier Roblin argued that, in effect, Manitoba had become a third-class province, inferior to the original four in not controlling natural resources, and inferior to the newer prairie provinces by being restricted to only a fraction of its potential inheritance and by having inadequate federal compensation for federal control of natural resources.

The Liberal government in Ottawa made it clear that it had rewarded Saskatchewan and Alberta because they were Liberal, and that it would do the same for Manitoba. But the threat was counterproductive, for Roblin accepted the challenge and helped defeat the Liberal Government of Laurier in 1911. He received a knighthood, and Manitoba acquired 180,000 miles of bush and tundra, full control of the rivers flowing to Hudson Bay, a good stretch of the Bay shoreline, geographic equality with the other prairie provinces, and untold mineral wealth.

It was particularly unfortunate that the boundary issue had not been settled earlier and that it was finally settled on political lines, for the main issue in the 1911 federal election was low tariffs. Roblin and Manitoba had a choice between the federal Conservatives, who offered fair boundaries, and the federal Liberals, who promised low tariffs. Both policies were extremely valuable to Manitoba. But borders would be permanent, low tariffs might not, and Manitoba broke with the other prairie provinces by electing federal Conservatives. Laurier had sealed his own defeat by refusing to give Manitoba the same northern border he had voluntarily given Alberta and Saskatchewan, a concession that would have cost the federal government nothing. Thus, Manitoba politics played a key role in two of the most important federal elections, that of 1896 which brought Laurier to power and that of 1911 which ended his fifteen-year reign.

Roblin's successes enabled his government to win five elections between 1900 and 1914. Yet unavoidably, with the accomplishments went the failures, such as the inability to solve the grain-handling and elevator problems. With age came increasing conservatism, and the government failed to respond to rising reformist issues such as women's suffrage and temperance. As support eroded, Roblin's government resorted to increasingly corrupt practices in order to cling to power, and actually won its last election with fewer popular votes than the Opposition obtained. This government was finally laid low by that most venerable of Canadian institutions, the public works scandal.

By 1912 it was obvious that the old legislative buildings were inadequate for a province of Manitoba's status and aspirations. Contracts
were let for what was and still is one of the finest public buildings in
Canada. Although no one expected the government to reward its
enemies, the public nevertheless became concerned at the rumours of
graft, corruption, kickbacks, overpricing, undelivered goods, wages to
non-existent workers, the building of mansions out of materials from
the construction site, and other examples of transfer of wealth from
public purse to party faithful. The official Liberal Opposition forced an
inquiry, which found the government innocent. That led to further
charges of a cover-up, of evidence withheld or destroyed, and of wit-
nesses unaccountably absent.

The government was forced to appoint a Royal Commission, to clarify
its terms of reference, and to appoint independent and capable commissioners. It took little time for the government and the contractors to be
found guilty of defrauding the public. The Conservatives and Liberals
then made a backroom deal whereby the Conservatives would resign,
the Liberal leader Tobias Norris would become Premier, and the scandal
would be forgotten. A thoroughly aroused public forced a continuation
of the investigation. This revealed corruption on other government
contracts, in the purchase of land, and in that bottomless pork-barrel,
the Highways Department. The political careers of the Conservatives
involved were ruined, but, beyond this, they were never punished. The
main contractor, Kelly, repaid $30,000 of the missing $1,200,000 and
spent less than his minimum sentence at Stoney Mountain Penitentiary,
not working at hard labour but rather as a "guest" of the warden.

In effect, the Roblin Government had caused its own defeat, as its
predecessor had done. But the Liberals had also contributed to that
defeat by developing a political platform which contrasted sharply with
Conservative policies and gave the people a clear alternative. Their
platform was simply reform, which particularly appealed to the richer
farmers, to Anglo-Saxons, to women, and to the sophisticated urban
voters. True to their word, the election of 1915 ushered in a long-
overdue period of change, and the Norris Government proved to be one
of the few governments in Manitoban history truly dedicated to reform.
This reform movement was part of a broader North American development known as the Progressive Movement, but it was moulded for
Manitoba's circumstances by the new Liberal Government.

Politics experienced one of its periodic cleansings, with new electoral
laws that sharply reduced the opportunities for political corruption.
Paradoxically, there was an undemocratic aspect to this reform, for it

weakened the political influence of the ethnic bloc, a group that had not quite learned how to play the game by Anglo-Saxon rules. It is possible that a little prejudice was mixed in with the idealism of the government and its supporters. The Civil Service Commission was established to ensure that the bureaucracy was recruited on the basis of merit rather than patronage. This undoubtedly improved the quality of government, but made it less representative of the rural, the poor, and the ethnic parts of the province. It was an admirable ideal; it was also self-serving for the educated Anglo-Saxon urban elite. A few ultra-democratic ideas were borrowed from the American Progressive Movement, such as the right of the people to draft and pass legislation by themselves, an idea quickly declared unconstitutional by the courts.

Primary education was made compulsory, and English was made the sole language of instruction. The latter was perhaps a necessary reform, for with ethnic schools graduates were appearing who could speak neither English nor French. Manitoba entered the Age of Welfare, with mother's allowances, assistance for widows, and workmen's compensation. Other reforms included safety legislation for factories, better labour laws, and more assistance for agricultural research. In 1916 the Norris Government became the first in Canada to grant women the vote. As early as 1893 a petition for women's suffrage had gained five thousand signatures. By 1910 the movement had come to maturity led by one of the most remarkable women in Canadian history, Nellie McClung, whose satirical plays rendered forever absurd the idea that men should monopolize politics. By 1920 a woman had been elected to the legislature and their influence began to be felt in the political life of the province.

The influence of women's suffrage was soon especially evident in the triumph of temperance, a movement to which it was inextricably linked. The origins of this crusade are found essentially in Christian theology. Temperance appealed particularly to the influential Presbyterians, who believed that drinking and partying were evil. Those who found "demon rum" an affront to civilization could have asked for no greater challenge than Western Canada at the turn of the century. Many of the settlers—Celtic, Scandinavian, Slavic, and southern German—came from societies where alcohol was acceptable and excessive drinking all too common. Many of them had always made their own liquor and continued to do so. These people found themselves on the frontier where the work was endless, rewards inadequate, frustration constant, where men greatly outnumbered women, and where there was little to while away any spare time. Beer eased the summer's heat, whiskey the winter's cold.

Drinking was unquestionably one of the most serious problems in the West. Numerous stories attest to the evils of drunkenness, of fighting and gambling and alcoholism, of accidents, absenteeism, and loss of jobs, of farmers who drank part of the harvest money, workers whose weekend binge left the family short of food before next payday, and of miners and loggers who lost a winter's wages in a weekend in Winnipeg's infamous Red Light district.

The campaign against the liquor trade began before 1900 and expanded throughout the period of prosperity. The War gave temperance its final impetus, for how could men be allowed to drink in idleness when the soldiers were dying in France? It triumphed in the 1915 election when the Anglo-Saxon Protestants of Greenway replaced the ethnic-supported government of Roblin. In 1916 the liquor trade was abolished, and the evils associated with it declined immediately.

Liquor did not disappear from the province. It could be obtained from any drugstore with a doctor's prescription, and diseases of epidemic proportions soon appeared which only brandy could cure. The drugstores and doctors could not fill the demand, so bootleggers appeared, illegally selling good liquor supplemented by moonshiners selling home brew. The old problems caused by excessive drinking began to reappear along with some new ones. Since it was illegal, the liquor trade created crime. Prohibition often made hypocrites out of doctors, druggists, police, and the courts, and bred a general disrespect for the law. Europeans who had come to Canada in search of freedom found that it was illegal to have a drink with a friend, something unheard of in the otherwise oppressive societies they had fled. There could be no age limit to something totally illegal, so teenage drinking became a problem. Since home brew was not inspected, some of it had devastating effects on the nervous system, stomach, and liver.

By 1923 the government had realized its error. The problem was not liquor but excessive drinking; the solution was not abolition but government control of the excesses. Compromise legislation was introduced which would permit some social drinking but severely limited the amount anyone could purchase at one time and made public drinking as unenjoyable as possible. The evolution toward rational social customs and laws had begun, but the temperance league fought such a bitter rearguard action that even by the 1970s some of the unpleasant and restrictive laws of the prohibition era were still in force.

The Unprogressive Era 1918—1930

Shortly after the First World War a statue called the Golden Boy was mounted on the dome of the newly-completed legislative building facing the last frontier, the North. It was to be the symbol of the golden era, of the promise of a great future for the province. But the golden era was already over. The unique combination of circumstances that had created the unprecedented prosperity of the first two decades of the Twentieth Century suddenly disappeared. Winnipeg and Manitoba descended gradually into a relative decline. The first symptoms were the Winnipeg General Strike and agrarian protest. The unprogressive era had begun.

While agriculture progressed in the early years of the century, industry also developed in Winnipeg. With it came trade unions pressing for the usual package of reforms: higher wages, shorter hours, and better working conditions. From an early date they sensed that neither the Liberal nor the Conservative party was to be their champion. As early as 1894 Winnipeg had a Trade and Labour Council and in 1900 the Independent Labour Party elected a Member of Parliament to Ottawa. Both Social Democratic and Socialist parties were being organized in the early 1900s. Their goals ranged from the simple humanitarian desire to improve the lot of the working poor by political pressure, to the Marxist belief that this could only be achieved by destroying the whole capitalist system.

As the wartime boom turned factory owners into millionaires, so too it greatly strengthened organized labour. Throughout the war, patriotism was exploited by government and management to increase production, keep down wages, and discourage strikes. By 1918 there was much pent-up frustration in the ranks of labour. The Russian Revolution supposedly offered the example of the transfer of power from the few to the many, an example which encouraged labour and frightened the wealthy. As the war moved to its climax labour relations began to deteriorate, and trouble erupted between the City of Winnipeg and its employees and between some companies and their metal workers. In both cases the threat of a strike preceeded a settlement. Then the war boom ended and the factories began laying off workers just as the soldiers were returning from Europe. This fall in the demand for labour, combined with an increase in the supply, created the type of labour surplus that business had often exploited to drive down wages and break labour organizations.

In particular the companies wanted to use the situation to prevent labour from obtaining or strengthening the right of collective bargaining. Labour was equally determined to maintain that right for without it the companies could pay different wages for the same type of work, play employees off against each other, break the unions, and reduce wages. Labour trouble began on May 1. The immediate question was, as usual, wages and hours, but the real issue was collective bargaining. If labour lost that strike all unions would suffer, so on May 15, after a 7:1 vote, the Winnipeg General Strike began.

Essential services were maintained, but the city was effectively shut down. The labour leaders forbade demonstrations and an eerie quiet descended on the city. Little happened for a month. Tempers began to fray, patience was dissipated, city, provincial, and federal governments dithered, and the police searched in vain for the Communist agents who existed mainly in their imaginations and in the propaganda of the companies. Gradually more and more workers admitted defeat and began drifting back to work. Negotiations resumed; the strike was failing.

Suddenly the federal government precipitated a crisis. It arrested the labour leaders and then realeased them. Naturally both they and the strikers wanted to meet to discuss the situation. But the city government forbade mass meetings. The meeting took place anyway—how could anyone have thought it would not? The Riot Act was read and police armed with pistols and clubs attacked the unarmed crowd. One man was killed, another died later of injuries. The Winnipeg General Strike had been broken.

Some of the leaders were imprisoned on the dubious charge of seditious conspiracy. Their ordeal, trials, and prison sentences served as the basis for several political careers. One of the leaders, John Queen, was elected Mayor of Winnipeg; another, the Reverend J.S. Woodsworth, went on to found the Cooperative Commonwealth Federation (CCF), the forerunner of the New Democratic Party. In 1920 some of these men were elected to the Provincial Assembly while still in prison. Four foreigners were deported for no other reason than that they were foreigners. Winnipeg's radical reputation was established, and north Winnipeg has voted leftist ever since. The strike weakened labour for decades, and though the right to collective bargaining was retained, the unfortunate impression was created that the strike was the only way to achieve the basic rights of labour. Yet although labour may have been broken, the farmers were just rising to power.

The farmers faced a situation after the war as critical as that of the workers. The European market for Canadian wheat collapsed, as Europe simply could not afford imports. The world supply of wheat increased rapidly as European production resumed, there were a number of excellent harvests, and Latin American wheat again entered world trade. The war had exhausted the accumulated capital of Europe, capital which had fuelled two decades of world prosperity. The price of wheat therefore fell dramatically, but the costs to the farmer of machinery, transportation, fuel, and consumer goods receded little from wartime highs, and his standard of living fell precipitously. The farmers' predicament was worsened rather than alleviated by post-war federal policies, for the government abandoned the control of grain-marketing which had brought stability to wheat prices. The farmers rose in revolt, a revolt that was to determine the course of Manitoban politics for the next four decades.

The history of agrarian protest in Manitoba dates from at least the 1880s when the first settlers protested against inadequate railway, elevator, and storage facilities, high freight rates, the deliberate under-grading of wheat by the grain companies, high tariffs, and high interest rates. They protested, too, against the governments which failed to solve these problems. In 1883 the Manitoba and North-West Farmers' Union was organized to advocate a solution to these grievances. The two main parties did not respond sufficiently to this pressure, and within a decade the farmers had elected two of their own candidates to the Provincial Assembly.

In the early 1900s criticism of the inadequacies of the grain companies quickly mounted. The farmers organized the Grain Growers' Association and, when all other forms of pressure failed, elected their own candidate to the House of Commons. Their Association forced the provincial government to purchase a line of elevators in order to introduce some competition into the business. Yet the government bungled the attempt, the result of a lack of conviction, patronage, mismanagement, and political interference. The government had failed them, so the farmers decided to solve the problem themselves. They leased the government elevators, built more, erected enormous elevators at Thunder Bay, opened offices abroad, and amalgamated with other prairie organizations to form their own giant company, the United Grain Growers. It has been a feature of the Canadian economy and of the landscape ever since. Wartime prosperity, government co-operation, and the patriotism induced by the wartime effort suppressed farm agitation. But when all the pre-war grievances surfaced in 1919-1920 the farmers quickly decided to act independently rather than through the two existing parties. It was a decision of momentous consequences, for the West has been dominated by third parties for much of the period since then. In fact, three of these Western parties—the Progressives, the CCF (NDP), and the Social Credit—spread to other provinces and into federal politics. The question must be asked: since their grievances had existed for two generations, why did the farmers suddenly abandon the old two-party political tradition of Canada, Britain, and the United States?

In the eyes of Westerners, Conservatives and Liberals had always represented the interests of Eastern Canada in such matters as tariffs, railways, and banking. The West, being new and having large immigrant populations, has often been more innovative and less conservative than Central Canada and especially the Maritimes. Among the immigrant groups was the American minority, many of whom came from an agrarian frontier where third-party protest was well developed. The economy of the West was based on the farmer, and more than any other group the farmers had a tradition of organization for co-operative endeavour, from community barn-building to massive organization for selling wheat. The 1911 federal election hurt both major parties in the West—the Conservatives for endorsing higher tariffs, the Liberals for failing to win re-election on an issue favourable to the West. The First World War further weakened the Conservatives, who, at the federal level, introduced conscription, a policy that was resented by farmers facing an acute manpower shortage and by the large ethnic population which did not identify with the English cause. The three provincial Conservative parties went into decline for more than a generation. The war weakened the Liberals equally, for the three provincial Liberal parties split with the federal party and supported the national Conservative-Unionist Government.

The farmers' dislike of federal parties spilled over into the provincial arena. By the 1920s farmers were tired of seeing both Liberal and

Conservative provincial parties support their national counterparts in policies harmful to their and Manitoba's interests. They were tired of seeing politics dominated by lawyers. They were tired of what they perceived to be Winnipeg's domination of provincial politics. And they were tired of labour, especially problems like the Winnipeg General Strike. They were not particularly unhappy with the Norris Government, which had implemented many of the reforms they wanted, but they opposed its high level of expenditure and had been unable to make Norris change that policy. Finally, and most importantly, they were tired of the workings of a political system which had failed to respond to their needs and had thwarted their demands.

In the 1920 election, farmers nominated candidates in twenty-six of the fifty-six constituencies. They ran as individual members who would vote for the legislation they liked and against everything else. They would not vote according to the discipline of a party controlled in Winnipeg, Toronto, or Ottawa. They won twelve seats, and could have formed a majority had they contested every riding. The Norris Government was reduced to a minority. Although they constituted the second largest group in the Assembly, the farmers refused to form the Opposition, thus effectively destroying the two-party system and achieving one of their goals.

The Norris Government staggered on, but its position was untenable. After defeat in the Assembly, it called another election. This time farmer candidates ran in most ridings and they won a majority, the opposition being divided almost equally among four groups. Leaderless, they beseeched the President of the Agricultural College, John Bracken, to become their premier. With no political background whatsoever, Bracken became Manitoba's most successful politician, being Premier from 1922 until 1943. His lack of partisanship was revealed by easy shifts from United Farmer to Progressive to Liberal to Conservative. He was a colourless, honest, able administor, a non-drinking moralist who banned smoking in the Assembly and introduced film censorship. His support was based largely on the Anglo-Saxon farmers of South-West Manitoba and on small businessmen, but the success of his party owed much to the massive over-representation of the countryside (one farm vote equalled two urban ones) and to divisions in the ethnic vote.

Once in office the paradox of a radical farmers' government became apparent. When driven to the limits of frustration by a particular grievance, famers became quite radical. Yet beneath that single-issue radicalism, and in good times, they were among the most conservative groups in Canada. The fundamentally conservative nature of this so-called Progressive Government was shown in its attitude toward finances. It abandoned one of the most "progressive" policies of previous Liberal and Conservative governments, namely massive borrowing for investment in the economy. Instead, it adopted the most conservative of fiscal policies, the balanced budget. To achieve this the government introduced an income tax, the first step in a still-continuing struggle to shift the burden of taxes from land to income. This reform very clearly represented the personal interests of farmers, for the entire income of wage earners, but not that of farmers, could be subject to the income tax. Expenditure on welfare, pensions, schools, and hospitals was reduced, as was the size of the civil service. This unwillingness to increase taxes or to borrow meant that there was little money available for innovation—for thirty years hardly one new program was launched, the government being satisfied that it was filling its mandate merely by administering the programs it had inherited. Education, both secondary and university, desperately needed support—the provincial government provided little. In effect, it had no education policy. It did legalize the liquor trade, mainly to increase revenue, but it then imposed as many nasty regulations as possible to make the consumption of liquor uncomfortable and unpleasant.

In one important respect, though, the Bracken Government did continue the expansionist policies of its predecessors. That was in the provision of an infrastructure for the development of the province's economy. The government continued building roads and expanding railways into the mining and forest region east of Lake Winnipeg where it also supported the development of the pulp and paper industry. The enormous mineral wealth discovered at Flin Flon could not be exploited until a railway was constructed. Bracken supported the building of a branch from the Hudson Bay Railway, thus ensuring that Flin Flon would be in the economic hinterland of Manitoba rather than that of Saskatchewan. Private capital was left to develop the mine. The Hudson Bay Mining and Smelting Company was born, and Flin Flon became one of Canada's greatest mining centres.

Bracken also supported the development of hydro-electric power at Seven Sisters on the Winnipeg River, which gave Manitoba cheap electricity for decades. These measures reflected Bracken's personal determination to diversify the economy and open up the north. Unfortunately, he could not completely overcome the attitude of his supporters —his government spent less in these areas than had its predecessors and it clearly favoured less government intervention in the economy than had the governments of Roblin and Norris. And, paradoxically for a farmers' government elected primarily to solve agricultural problems, Manitoba was the only prairie province that did not support the establishment of a national wheat marketing board.

In one other way the Progressive Government was reactionary, namely in its attitude to labour. In this its history reveals a paradox of Canadian political history and especially of Canadian political theory. Both farmer and worker emerged from the First World War with major grievances. Labour launched the Winnipeg General Strike; the farmers launched the Progressive Movement. Both were attempts to change the *status quo*, and they shared such enemies as big business, the wealthy, and the federal government. An assumption arose that there was a community of interest between farmer and worker, an assumption that owes more to socialist ideology than to Canadian political experience, but which has long survived.

The Progressive era in Manitoba taught otherwise, for the interests of farmer and worker were opposed and the farmers' government spent decades thwarting the interests of labour. Basically the farmer wanted the maximum price for the food the worker consumed and the minimum price for the goods and services the worker produced. The worker wanted the opposite—cheap food and high wages. The political alliance that did make sense, and the one that was the true basis of the farmers' government, was between farmers and small and local businessmen. The profits earned by Manitoban businessmen were a small fraction of the farmers' costs, and were likely to be re-invested in the towns and cities that served the farmer and with which he identified. Local merchants extended credit in hard times and faced bankruptcy together with their clients, many of whom they knew personally. The farmer and the businessman had a common interest in small government, low taxes, low wages, cheap manufactured goods, low freight rates, free trade, and even in a railway to Hudson Bay. In 1920 farmers and businessmen formed a coalition aimed against the interests of workers and the city of Winnipeg. It did not have to do anything to implement this policy—it achieved its aim by simply doing nothing. For thirty years the Government of Manitoba did relatively little to promote the development of industry in the province or to assist the workers in the few industries that did exist or came to locate in the province.

Thus the decade of the 1920s opened with the joint protests of worker and farmer. But the workers were defeated, and the farmers, with the support of local businessmen, took over the province and ushered in decades of small-"c" conservative government which was misnamed "progressive". It was an understandable but unfortunate development. The grievances of the farmers could only be settled at the federal level, and there the two old parties prevailed. The government citadel the farmers had conquered could do little for them, so it did little. With the onslaught of the Depression, it did even less.

Quiet Depression, Quiet Surrender 1930–1955

The basic conservatism of the farmers' government, misnamed the Progressive Government, was heavily reinforced by the events of the 1930s, particularly the Depression. The 1930s can be seen as a watershed in Manitoba's history; as a period when optimism finally gave way to pessimism, when local innovation all but ceased, when a province which had repeatedly challenged national companies and the federal government abandoned provincial rights for federal grants and willingly restricted the scope of its responsibility. In this period Manitoba ceased to be one of the greatest opponents of Ottawa and became instead one of the champions of strong federal government, a trend that was at complete variance with what was happening in the other prairie provinces.

The Depression was the main factor that changed Manitobans from optimists to realists and finally to pessimists. It was one of the worst economic periods in history, and worse on the prairies than in the rest of Canada because man and nature simultaneously produced an economic recession and an agricultural drought. The former had a psychological cause—people simply stopped spending money. When they did, the stock market crashed, investment dried up, companies laid off workers, governments reduced spending as tax revenues declined, and international trade disintegrated as each country sought to protect its domestic market. Prices, particularly of agricultural products, declined sharply, and unemployment jumped to unprecedented levels. Married men who had always supported their families with pride were forced to go cap in hand to the city or municipal government for welfare; single men left homes and schools to ride the freight trains from coast to coast in search of any kind of work.

At the same time the prairies entered one of the worst dry spells in history. Beginning in 1929, precipitation in both winter and summer was woefully inadequate. Crops burned up in the record-setting heat waves, the soil turned to dust and blew away. Parts of the prairies that should never have been farmed turned into desert. Man thus added the dust storm to the catalogue of natural disasters, and nature reinforced the hardship by producing extremes of winter cold and summer heat. The international price of wheat sank to the lowest level in centuries so that the crops that did grow were hardly worth selling. The economy of the prairie provinces collapsed; the social fabric began to disintegrate; and the people were caught in a vicious circle of economic and agricultural disaster they could neither understand nor affect. People simply waited it out, scratching a sustenance living from the soil, amusing themselves as best they could, and waiting for next year.

The effects of the Depression on the prairies were then exaggerated rather than eased by federal policies. The federal government had to devalue the Canadian dollar, and it had two choices. Eighty cents US would make Central Canadian exports competitive; sixty cents was the required level for Western agricultural exports. The level was set at eighty cents, without even an attempt to compromise between the two rates. To protect Central Canadian industry from competition the tariff rates were increased, adding to the costs of consumer goods in the West without creating any new markets for Western products. The prairie provinces were being squeezed into bankruptcy by the combined effects of natural disaster, man-made depression, and the policies of the federal government.

The Depression led to the beginning of third-party politics in the other two prairie provinces, the Social Credit and the CCF rising to prominence in Alberta and Saskatchewan respectively, both of them dedicated in their own way to revolutionary change in the basic structure of Canadian capitalism. In Manitoba the basic conservatism of the government was reinforced. The same situation on the prairies had produced totally different responses, and it is essential to understand why Manitoba became reactionary instead of revolutionary. For one thing the basic population was quite different from that of Alberta and Saskatchewan. It was a generation older and was drawn more from Ontario and less from Eastern Europe and the United States, both of which were more radical. After fifty years of struggle the pioneering spirit of the people had been burned out, blunted by the successful solution of some problems and the apparent irrevocability of some others. Increasingly, new ideas came from the more recently arrived foreigners, but such ideas fell on the barren soil of the Anglo-Saxon farmers and the Anglo-Saxon elite that governed the province.

In Manitoba the more progressive elements of the population lived in Winnipeg, but the electoral system was deliberately designed to weaken if not destroy the influence of that city in provincial politics. With less than one-quarter of the Legislative seats, Winnipeg was greatly under-represented in government. Also, Winnipeg was a multi-seat constituency based on the principle of proportional representation, so that its representatives were hopelessly divided between Conservatives, Liberals, Labour, Progressives, Socialists, and Independents.

The failure of the Hudson Bay Railway (HBRR) reinforced conservatism. It was the sort of problem that eventually reduced the most aggressive and energetic prairie politician to despair. A railway from the prairies to Hudson Bay is hundreds of miles shorter than one to the Atlantic ports; the distance from Churchill to Europe shorter than that from Montreal. Compared to a railway to Vancouver the HBRR was also hundreds of miles shorter, avoided the Rockies, and the port of Churchill was thousands of miles closer to Europe than Vancouver. It should have been cheaper to ship wheat through Churchill than from any other Canadian port, just as it had always been cheaper to ship the furs through the Bay. Such a route should also have created competition with the east-west routes and forced a lowering of all freight rates.

The HBRR was first demanded by Manitobans in 1881. From then on it was the subject of constant pressure on the federal government, political parties, and railway companies. Promises were made, and little by little the railway crept northward into the bush and tundra. By 1890 forty miles of track had been laid; by 1910 it was at The Pas; by 1917 at Kettle Rapids and the beginning of the Hudson Bay Lowlands. In 1924 the "On to the Bay Association" was founded. In 1925 many farmers voted for the federal Progressive Party which made completion of the railway a price for its support for Mackenzie King's minority Liberal Government. By 1931 the HBRR was completed and wheat was being shipped at rates substantially below those from Montreal or Vancouver and the farmer, of course, gained the difference between those rates. Then the major insurance companies decided that the route was too dangerous and raised the insurance rates to equal the fall in freight rates. A half-century of tireless effort had finally produced a railway to the Bay, but it was all in vain. It should have been a major victory for the West. Instead it accomplished almost nothing. Another farmers' dream had died. For the farmers no political solution had worked. Politics had become hopeless.

The decline of Winnipeg was another cause of pessimism in Manitoba. From 1896 until 1913 Winnipeg had experienced unprecedented growth, becoming the largest city on the prairies, the third largest in Canada, the "Chicago of the North". It was a city destined to become, so its citizens believed, the largest and most important metropolis in Canada. Yet by 1913 it had begun to decline as a major Canadian metropolis, to be passed by Vancouver and to become merely the least dynamic of Canada's secondary cities such as Edmonton, Calgary, Hamilton, or Ottawa. Winnipeg's tremendous pre-war growth had depended on an unusual combination of circumstances—unprecedented world prosperity, a high level of free trade, an unnatural era of peace, the free movement of capital, massive immigration into the prairies, and tremendous European demand for Canadian foodstuffs. The First World War ended this golden era, seemingly forever, and other changes in the post-war period added to the decline.

As a distribution centre Winnipeg had been given freight rate advantages over other western cities. As the latter grew in political importance they were able to force gradual alterations so that slowly Winnipeg lost its preferred position, and its share of the western wholesale trade declined. The gradual population shift from small towns and villages to larger towns affected Winnipeg, for the village stores had tended to buy in Winnipeg, but those of the larger towns bought in sufficient quantity to order directly from Toronto or Montreal. Equally important was the opening of the Panama Canal in 1914, for it diverted half the trade of the prairies to Vancouver, and that city grew at Winnipeg's expense.

At the same time Winnipeg's entrepreneurial skills and free enterprise spirit fell victim to a vicious circle. Having failed so often, and facing such odds in fighting climate, geography, and provincial and federal politicians, businessmen became among the most conservative in Canada, so that real opportunities were either lost or left to immigrants and foreign investors. Capitalism, which had once benefitted the city, began to work against its interests. One tendency of capitalism is the concentration of capital and ownership. In the Canada of 1900 there were thousands of small, locally-owned factories and financial institutions. Gradually these had been amalgamated into giant Canadian firms or foreign-dominated corporations. At one time breweries, banks, meat-packing plants, pulp mills, and a variety of factories and businesses were owned by Winnipeggers, and the city benefitted from the presence of an energetic, risk-taking, decision-making class. As Toronto, Montreal, and foreign firms took over the Winnipeg plants, that class either left, become nominal vice presidents, or accepted a safe salary instead of the risks and rewards of capitalism. Part of the spirit of Winnipeg died with them. In short, Winnipeg not only declined relative to other Canadian cities and prairie centres, but there was a noticeable decline in energy, creativity, initiative, and independence. Although it remained the most dynamic part of the province, it was so under-represented politically that it ceased to have much influence on the political direction of the province.

Another development that took the steam out of provincial politics was the final solution to the Crown lands or natural resources issue. By 1930 the railways had been built and almost all land settled. The federal government no longer had an argument for retaining control of natural resources, and Manitoba and the other prairie provinces were finally raised to equality with the other six provinces. Thus the fourth of the bitterest issues in federal-provincial relations—railways, borders, schools, and Crown lands—was solved, and Manitoba no longer had cause to be one of the strongest provincial opponents of the central government.

All these factors reinforced the basic conservative nature of Bracken's Liberal-Progressive Government. Accordingly, it responded in a negative and unimaginative fashion to the crisis that befell the province in 1930. As agriculture and industry ground to a halt, tax revenue fell. Bracken immediately reduced government expenditure in an attempt to balance the budget. As local taxes declined the municipal governments had less and less revenue to face the mounting costs of relief. Eventually many went bankrupt and their welfare costs had to be assumed by the provincial government. Bracken increased welfare expenditure, but he financed it by cancelling capital projects, cutting spending in other areas, and reducing civil service salaries. Repeated appeals to the federal government led to a grudging and inadequate increase in federal grants. The federal government devised job-creating projects, providing the province paid half the costs. At great expense they provided work for a few, nothing for the majority, and tied up scarce provincial funds in projects designed in Ottawa for national objectives. Each project represented a loss of provincial independence, limiting still further the scope for provincial action and affecting negatively the attitudes of provincial politicians and civil servants to their jobs.

By 1933 the province was rapidly approaching bankruptcy. The federal government provided funds, but only on condition that the province do everything possible to balance the budget. The Cabinet was forced to consider closing schools, abolishing pensions, and discontinuing relief, proposals that were rejected as society would have collapsed. The 1933 budget raised taxes to the highest level in North America and reduced expenditure to the lowest possible level. At last the balanced budget was achieved, the credit rating maintained. These measures, unfortunate but necessary, ensured a continuation of bank loans and federal grants, and the Manitoba Government was able to survive the remaining six years of the Depression without going bankrupt. But the social cost was appalling. Tens of thousands of decent people were reduced to destitution. Rural families lived on rabbit and gopher stew, urban ones on hand-outs; people wore clothes until they fell apart and huddled together in the only room they could afford to heat.

Bracken eventually began to question the entire foundation of a political and economic system which forced one part of the country to bear a disproportionate share of the burden of depression. After thirteen years as Premier, including five years during the Depression, he began to identify a basic flaw in Canadian Confederation. Under the British North America Act tariffs were a federal responsibility, but corporate and personal income taxes, unemployment, and welfare were provincial. Herein lay the problem. The federal government had used its power over tariffs to launch the National Policy, which had led to the development of Canadian industry. Although this industry was located essentially in Ontario and Quebec, the products were sold throughout Canada and citizens from coast to coast supported this industry by paying a higher price for the goods they consumed. This would have lowered their standard of living at any time, but was particularly devastating during a depression. The burden of tariffs fell particularly on the West, which had little local industry to protect and sold its goods on the highly competitive world market. In a depression the West could not sell its products internationally, yet still had to pay the tariff-protected prices for products it purchased. This helped to reduce hundreds of thousands of people to unemployment and welfare. Under the British North America Act, relief was a provincial matter, and the burden fell precisely on those governments least able to support it.

For seven decades the West had campaigned unsuccessfully to lower the tariffs. Bracken saw no future in that battle. Instead he proposed that the government which had responsibility for tariffs should also have responsibility for both the problems created by those tariffs and for the revenue that came from them. From 1936 on Bracken advocated the transfer of unemployment and relief from provincial to federal jurisdiction. He did so in letters to other politicians, in articles for newspapers across the land, in speeches from Calgary to Montreal, and in a number of conferences, some of which he hosted.

Bracken began to urge the federal government to launch an inquiry into the whole nature of the federal system. The federal government eventually responded, setting up the Rowell-Sirois Royal Commission, with John Dafoe, the influential editor of the Winnipeg Free Press, as one of the main Commissioners. It launched the most thorough study of Canada ever undertaken. Manitoba submitted the most articulate and detailed brief, one of the only ones to make major and positive proposals for a solution to Canada's problems. The brief stated that the federal government should assume all the cost of relief and half the cost of mothers' allowances, hospitalization, health care, highways, and technical education.

The federal government refused to act on the recommendations of the Rowell-Sirois report. A majority of the government's support came from the industrial heartland of Canada, but it avoided the problem of implementing the recommendations of the Rowell-Sirois report by arguing that major changes in Confederation should not be made in wartime. Bracken failed in his effort to change the Canadian constitution, and reverted to attempts to broaden his coalition in Manitoba and to gain more Western support for his ideas. His provincial government continued in its conservative ways, a result of both financial stringency and unshakeably conservative attitudes. In 1943 Bracken, who had established a national reputation, assumed the leadership of the federal Progressive Conservative Party, at which he was a dismal failure. He was replaced by Stuart Garson, who was Premier from 1943 to 1948.

Nevertheless, Bracken was ultimately more successful than practically any other Canadian politician in correcting a fundamental flaw in Confederation. In 1940 the federal government amended the constitution to take responsibility for unemployment, which had virtually ceased to be a problem with the wartime boom. Soon after the war Ottawa assumed a larger share of the responsibility for assisting with the burdens caused by its tariff policy. Eventually it gained partial control of corporate and income taxes so that all Canadians benefitted from the industry created by the tariffs. By the 1960s equalization payments to the poorer provinces were an accepted fact in Canada, and by early 1980 attempts were being made to enshrine the principle of equalization payments in the constitution.

Manitoba and the federal government unilaterally put into practice some of Bracken's suggestions. In 1941 the province surrendered income and corporate taxes for the duration of the war in return for equivalent subsidies and the federal assumption of relief debts or welfare. In 1946 Premier Garson surrendered to Ottawa Manitoba's rights to income, corporate, and inheritance taxes in return for $13,000,000 per year.

Of course the province was surrendering constitutional rights, privileges, and responsibilities. But getting rid of the duty of providing welfare in return for the sacrifice of virtually non-existent tax resources seemed like a good bargain. Also, federal government policies weakened Manitoba's economic independence during the Depression, so, to a degree, Manitoba was only abandoning formally what it had already lost in fact.

The general defeatism of the 1930s and 1940s was reflected in provincial elections. In the face of depression the government reduced expenditure and raised taxes. It lacked policies and ideas, let alone dreams or visions. Yet in the 1932 election it actually increased its representation from twenty-nine to thirty-eight seats. The provincial government did not even administer properly what was clearly in its sphere of responsibility, such as the University of Manitoba. There the books were not audited between 1925 and 1932. When they were finally checked, it was discovered that an administrator had lost almost $1,000,000 of University funds on the stock market. In 1937 the electorate weighed the government's sad record and returned it to office with a minority status. War then produced a spirit of co-operation, so the government easily won the next elections in 1942 and 1945. After the war it continued to administer its reduced mandate with neither imagination nor enthusiasm, obviously with the agreement of the people who returned it to office in 1949 and 1953 under Douglas Campbell, Premier from 1948 to 1958.

Throughout this period the government had broadened its coalition, absorbing all or part of the Liberal, Conservative, and Social Credit Parties. It thus reflected accurately the mood of the people who voted, but it did not reflect the enormous minority of the population that lived in Winnipeg. In rural areas politics were so pointless that many constituencies repeatedly returned candidates by acclamation and less than 50% of the electorate bothered to vote at all. The Progressives had always been devoted to non-partisan, group government and Bracken achieved this to a remarkable degree. Throughout the 1930s he argued that the Depression was not the time to engage in partisan debate. Such opposition as there was failed to produce any better ideas on how to solve the problems of the province. There was neither advantage nor real opportunity for an Opposition Party to develop a clear alternative policy or provoke public debate on the issues. Bracken and the farmers had succeeded in smothering politics, and the ultimate result was not a coalition of the best politicians united in tackling problems, but a government which could stay in power by doing virtually nothing.

The inadequacies of the government were fully exposed by its inability to deal with the disastrous Winnipeg flood of 1950. Thirty years of laissez-faire thinking, penny-pinching administration, and abandoning responsibilities to Ottawa had produced a government mentally incapable of dealing with a real crisis. A Red River flood takes weeks to reach Winnipeg, and the height of water can be predicted long in advance. Yet as the waters swept over town after town in their relentless advance, government preparations to save a city of 400,000 were woefully inadequate. When the flood struck, the government hesitated to proclaim an emergency, failed to provide sufficient resources, and could not agree on the amount of compensation to be paid. What was worse, it proved incapable of envisaging any sort of solution to the problem. Manitoba was entering the second half of the Twentieth Century with a government that still thought of itself as the non-political administrator of a large municipality, whose vision of its own responsibilities did not extend much beyond the administration of justice and the grading and gravelling of a few dirt roads.

Hope Revived
1955 — 1970

In the mid-1950s the Manitoba Government began to awaken from its deep slumber. The ease with which it had absorbed the potential political opposition ended when the Conservatives began to act like a political party instead of a faction to be bought off with one or two seats in Cabinet. A new political breeze was blowing through the province, as it was at the federal level where two decades of Liberal rule were drawing to a close. Manitoba businessmen began to realize that more was required of a provincial government than minimal taxes, a balanced budget, and careful administration. In fact, an increasing number of Manitobans began to realize how backward their province had become. This was obvious as soon as they drove onto the better roads in neighbouring provinces and states, obvious as soon as they compared educational facilities with those of Saskatchewan, Alberta, or Ontario, obvious to any traveller who compared the stagnation of Brandon, Selkirk, or Winnipeg to the dynamism of other towns and cities on the prairies.

The 1950s were a decade of social change, and that inevitably affected politics. Cars and trucks had appeared in numbers in the 1920s, but the Depression and the war had seriously retarded the transportation revolution. Now, in the early 1950s, the internal combustion engine definitely replaced the horse, and the government was forced to launch a road-building program. More cars and better roads created great social change as the horizon of peoples' lives rapidly expanded. The decline of the small town and village, which had begun early in the century, rapidly accelerated, and larger centres such as Virden, Minnedosa, and Morden began to expand for the first time in decades. People perceived that education and health services were inadequate, but the government, still essentially conservative, initiated studies instead of action. Increasingly, people chafed at the petty liquor laws that made it impossible for anyone to consume any form of alcohol in a restaurant or for a man to enjoy food, female companionship, music, dancing, or even a dart game in his pub—rules that encouraged drunkenness and fights more than they limited the consumption of alcohol. The government then appointed former Premier Bracken to study the liquor laws. This time it took action: on the basis of Bracken's recommendations, and against great opposition, it introduced reforms which made drunkenness more rare and social enjoyment more common.

Then, in a move that was democratic but suicidal, the government initiated electoral reform. By the mid-1950s Manitoba's constituencies bore little resemblance to the principle of representation by population. The government had been repeatedly returned to office with less than half of the votes cast and politics had become so pointless that almost half the population ceased to vote at all. Something had to be done, so, as with the liquor laws and health and education services, the government appointed a committee to study the problem.

Surprisingly, the government accepted the committee's recommendations. Winnipeg's representation was increased from 25% to 40% of the seats, giving the most dynamic part of the province a major influence on government policy for the first time in Manitoba's history. All constituencies were made single-member, which ended the hopeless splintering of the Winnipeg vote, and the constituency borders were redrawn on the basis of geographic and economic unity rather than the electoral advantage of the government. It was perhaps the most democratic electoral reform in Canadian political history, and it produced an electoral situation so closely attuned to political attitudes that a slight change in the mood of Manitobans can lead to a government's defeat. In fact, Manitoba governments have been defeated four times since then, in contrast to previous Manitoba history or normal Canadian practice where governments tend to remain in power for decades.

Politically the electoral reform was suicidal, but probably nothing could have saved the aged administration. Manitoba was changing and the government had to change with it. Yet the most dangerous time for any government is when it opens the floodgates of reform after years of conservatism. For a government long in power, reform carries the political danger of estranging its conservative support without attracting an equal number of votes from the progressive elements of the population, people who have possibly become alienated from the government and distrust its reformist intentions or regard them as death-bed repentence. This is precisely what happened in Manitoba in the mid-1950s. The changes in the liquor laws annoyed many supporters; the studies of education and health showed just how backward the province had become, and the electoral change aided the Opposition.

That Opposition, the Progressive Conservative Party, had recently acquired able political leadership for the first time since Rodmond Roblin resigned in 1916, and the new leader was his grandson, Dufferin. Under his direction the Conservatives began to act like a real political party. Debate in the Legislature became more meaningful. Constituencies that had returned candidates by acclamation suddenly experienced a competition between Government and Opposition candidates. Voters were faced with the unfamiliar responsibility of choosing between the conservative platform with the old candidates of the Government and the reform program of an Opposition which was increasingly staffed by the able candidates Roblin was attracting into public life.

In 1958 Roblin led his revived party to power, making a mockery of political labels, for his Conservative Government was far to the left of the Liberal-Progressive Government it replaced. In 1959 a new election produced a majority. The Roblin Government immediately tackled problems that had been neglected for years. The education system was shaken from top to bottom. Provincial grants and regulations resulted in a much-needed and long-overdue improvement in the quality of teachers. Against considerable opposition the consolidation of rural schools was carried out, producing a smaller number of larger schools capable of supporting the type of facilities previously known only in the cities. The Manitoba School Question was re-opened, and provincial aid given for the first time to Catholic schools. More aid would likely have cost Protestant votes without gaining an equivalent number of Catholic ones, so Roblin was forced to draw back from full financial support.

At the University, a combination of federal and provincial grants resulted in a vast expansion of facilities, partly to make up for previous neglect, partly to meet the incoming hordes of the wartime baby boom. The Anglican College of St. John's and the Catholic College of St. Paul's moved to the Fort Garry campus; Brandon College became a university; United College, the former Wesley College of the United Church, became the University of Winnipeg, a downtown campus offering competition to the University of Manitoba at Fort Garry. Health and welfare services were also greatly expanded, and new hospitals and senior citizens' homes became a feature of small towns across the province.

Problems common to most cities in the mid-Twentieth Century were beginning to afflict Winnipeg. The middle class was moving to the low-tax suburbs, leaving the core of the city with a reduced tax base on which to support the same burden of services, many of which were still used by the suburbanites. Roblin attacked the problem directly. Based on the principle that all of the urban populace used the basic services and should therefore pay taxes to support them, a single government was created for the entire metropolitan area. It instituted a uniform property tax, took over many services such as transportation, water, sewage, and parks, and provided a common approach to civil defence and flood protection. A uniform building and zoning code was devised to prevent the ugliness and lost revenue that occurs when tiny municipalities compete for scarce industry. None of Roblin's reforms were introduced without opposition, and as with any government which attempts to introduce change too quickly, mistakes were made aplenty. Both the opposition and the errors were evident in the urban program. Nevertheless, it was a good initial attack on one of the most intractable of modern problems.

In 1882 the CPR had made the mistake of locating the major prairie metropolis in Winnipeg where recurrent floods inflicted untold damage and restricted the city's development. For over a century Winnipeg had lived with the situation; sacrificing low-lying areas and desperately attempting to save the rest with dykes and ditches and volunteer sandbagging. Every spring produced anxiety; every few years there was a crisis; and the millions of dollars of damage of the famous 1950 flood made the situation intolerable. Roblin initiated a solution with imagination and vigour. In effect, a second river bed was dug from St. Norbert to Lockport, one of the largest earth-moving projects in history. Because there were no floods during the years of construction, people ridiculed "Duff's Ditch". The government's memory and foresight were more sound than that of the electorate—the Red River Floodway probably paid for itself in the single flood season of 1969.

The Roblin Government believed that Manitoba's frail economy required massive government intervention. In this belief it followed the tradition of Manitoba governments from 1870 to 1920, and was in sharp contrast to the laissez-faire attitude of the farmers' government. Attempts to attract and expand industry were launched, especially through the creation of the Manitoba Development Corporation. It was particularly dedicated to fostering small industry in the towns and cities outside Winnipeg in an attempt to preserve the small town, to balance economic development throughout the province, and to prevent

Winnipeg from totally dominating the economy. The government provided power, water, and industrial parks and connected these towns with a massive program of trunk-road construction, something the province had needed for years. The policy was complemented by full-scale development of the immense hydro potential of the Saskatchewan, Nelson, and Churchill Rivers. The Manitoba Development Corporation negotiated with private companies to bring them to the province, and provided tax concessions, grants, and low-interest loans to those that did. As a risk-raking organization it had, like private enterprise, its share of failures. These, and its necessary secrecy, were constantly criticized, but the Corporation's impact has been quite positive.

One of the industrial development projects was to become extremely controversial. The least developed part of the province was the North. There the burden of unemployment, under-employment, absence of steady jobs, poverty, and accompanying social dislocation fell precisely on the groups least able to adapt to modern society, the Indians and Metis. Above all, Roblin wanted economic development in this area. Lengthy, difficult, and frustrating negotiations failed to produce an attractive project to stimulate the economy of the area.

Eventually a deal was negotiated with a Swiss firm to establish a $1,000,000 pulp, paper, and wood products complex at The Pas. Manitoba put up the greater part of the capital for Churchill Forest Industries; the Swiss concern provided some capital, plus management and technology. Part of the project was successful, part was not. Costs for some aspects of the project such as consulting became excessive in the opinion of many critics, and money was allegedly drained from Manitoba to foreign companies. Political responsibility or credit for the successes and failures of the project came to be blurred when the Roblin Government was replaced by the NDP. The latter continued with the project, launching an investigation at the same time. The assignment of credit or blame is still a matter of partisan politics in Manitoba. The project was clearly not the social, economic, and political success the Roblin Government hoped for.

Manitobans were impressed with Roblin's achievements; they were also critical of the lack of development and disturbed by rumours about Churchill Forest Industries. Unfortunately for Roblin, Manitoba had become one of the most difficult Canadian provinces to govern. It was more difficult than the wealthier provinces where governments basked in the glow of economic success, more difficult than the poorer ones where conservatism, inertia, traditional voting patterns, and large transfers of federal funds allowed governments to remain in power for decades. In Manitoba the progressive and conservative elements of society were very evenly balanced, and with the electoral reforms of the 1950s, a slight change of opinion could have immediate effects on government fortunes. In 1958 Manitobans had voted for more progressive government, but that shift was heavily qualified. Manitobans were willing to take a few cautious steps toward the future, but successful politics depended on an extremely fine appreciation of just how middle-of-the-road Manitoba really was. Roblin had not misjudged that mood; he had gambled that quick economic development would change it.

When the hoped-for economic breakthrough failed to materialize, Roblin was forced to introduce a sales tax to help pay for the tremendous improvements he had brought. In his first election he had promised not to introduce such a tax, and although he had later qualified that promise, the electorate chose to hold him to it. When he left provincial politics to run for the federal Conservatives he was heavily defeated in a Winnipeg riding. He had tried to do too much too quickly and it had not paid off soon enough. He had moved too far in advance of public opinion. He was too progressive and not sufficiently conservative, and, in the best of democratic traditions, he paid the price. His successor, Walter Weir, relaxed the reformist drive of the Roblin Government and began consolidating and administering existing programs. Unfortunately, for Weir, the people still wished for the continuation of reform. After winning three by-elections Weir called a snap election hoping to catch the leaderless NDP off guard. But the NDP called an immediate leadership convention, elected the young and dynamic Edward Schreyer, and narrowly defeated the surprised Conservatives.

The 1969 election marked not only the first triumph of a neo-socialist party in Manitoba, but also the victory of the ethnic vote over the Anglo-Saxon, and of the north-east of the province over the south-west. Politicians from north Winnipeg sat on the government side of the Legislature for the first time since the Winnipeg General Strike, and Manitobans of German, French, and Ukranian ancestry held key Cabinet portfolios. Apart from nationalizing the automobile insurance business, the Schreyer Government introduced remarkably little in the way of new or radical legislation, being content to make major improvements in health and welfare and other existing programs. The press and public engaged in a great debate over free enterprise versus public ownership, but in fact the province had never known free enterprise and was not to experience real socialism. The question was not the existence of government intervention in the economy, which almost everyone accepted, but the degree of government interference. Ideologically, the Roblin

Conservatives had believed in a considerable degree of private enterprise, but they practised considerable government intervention. Ideologically the Schreyer NDP, and especially its left wing, preached the merits of massive government intervention, but in practice it differed remarkably little from Roblin's Government. Schreyer operated essentially in the tradition of gradual and progressive change and considerable government intervention, a tradition that had begun in the mid-1950s and, with the exception of the short and unrepresentative Weir Government, lasted at least until the NDP defeat in 1977.

It seems clear that as the 1970s drew to a close, Manitobans were still unsure of the type of government they required to reflect their particular history and population and to deal with the political and economic facts of their situation. More than any other province Manitoba is a microcosm of Canada, with English-Protestant majority and French-Catholic and ethnic minorities. It is urbanized, but has a solid rural and small-town population; heavily industrialized but with a mixed economy based on farming, fishing, forestry, minerals, energy resources, and the major service industries; with an old and established business community but an industrial base owned outside the province. Like the rest of Canada its economy is partly self-sufficient and partly dependent on the whims of the broader Canadian and world economies. As in any democracy its governments have reflected the changes in the composition and attitudes of its population and in its economic circumstances. At one time the greatest proponent of provincial rights, by the late 1930s the province had become one of the champions of strong central government, a situation that has not changed even though it sympathizes with the other Western provinces and even with Quebec. Essentially it is a have-not province which has suspected since the 1920s or 1930s that it would not attain the promise that seemed so real in 1900. Manitoba's capacity to affect its own destiny is sharply limited by geography, climate, its political situation, and its history. Nevertheless, within those limits it has achieved a measure of success and reached a level of culture and civilization of which all its citizens can be proud. That alone provides the hope that more can be achieved in the future.

Index